KOVELS'
Quick Tips

Books by Ralph and Terry Kovel

American Country Furniture 1780–1875

Dictionary of Marks—Pottery & Porcelain

A Directory of American Silver, Pewter and Silver Plate

Kovels' Advertising Collectibles Price List

Kovels' American Art Pottery: The Collector's Guide
to Makers, Marks, and Factory Histories

Kovels' American Silver Marks

Kovels' Antiques & Collectibles Fix-It Source Book

Kovels' Antiques & Collectibles Price List

Kovels' Book of Antique Labels

Kovels' Bottles Price List

Kovels' Collector's Guide to American Art Pottery

Kovels' Collector's Source Book

Kovels' Depression Glass & American Dinnerware
Price List

Kovels' Guide to Selling, Buying, and Fixing Your
Antiques and Collectibles

Kovels' Guide to Selling Your Antiques & Collectibles

Kovels' Illustrated Price Guide to Royal Doulton

Kovels' Know Your Antiques

Kovels' Know Your Collectibles

Kovels' New Dictionary of Marks—Pottery & Porcelain

Kovels' Organizer for Collectors

Kovels' Price Guide for Collector Plates, Figurines, Paperweights,
and Other Limited Editions

KOVELS'
Quick Tips

~ *799* ~

Helpful Hints

on How to

Care for Your

Collectibles

Ralph & Terry Kovel
Illustrations by Bob Dasher

CROWN TRADE PAPERBACKS   NEW YORK

Published by Crown Trade Paperbacks, 201 East 50th Street, New York, New York 10022. Member of the Crown Publishing Group.

Random House, Inc. New York, Toronto, London, Sydney, Auckland

CROWN TRADE PAPERBACKS is a trademark of Crown Publishers, Inc.

Manufactured in the United States of America

Design by Deborah Kerner and Mercedes Everett

Library of Congress Cataloging-in-Publication Data
Kovel, Ralph M.
  Kovels' quick tips : 799 helpful hints on how to care for your collectibles
/ Ralph and Terry Kovel.—1st ed.
  Includes index.
  1. Collectibles—Miscellanea. 2. Antiques—Collection and preservation—
Miscellanea. 3. Collectors and collecting—Miscellanea. I. Kovel, Terry H. II. Title.
AM231.K66   1995
790.1'12—dc20   95-6991
                                            CIP

ISBN 0-517-88381-3

10 9 8 7 6 5 4 3 2

Every book needs a dedication. This is dedicated to you, our readers. Without the thousands of letters we receive each month, this book would have been impossible.

Contents

Introduction ix
Advertising Collectibles 1
Aluminum 5
Animal Trophies 6
Architectural 8
Baseball Cards 9
Baskets 10
Books 11
Bottles 12
Brass 15
Bronze 17
Candlesticks and Candles 18
Carousels 20
Cartoons and Animation Cels 21
Chrome 22
Clocks 23
Collector Plates and Figurines 26
Copper 27
Dolls 28
Furniture 33
Games 49
Glass 50
Graniteware 56
Holiday 57
Iron 59
Ivory 60
Jewelry 62
Kitchen 68
Lacquer 71
Lamps 72

Leather 74
Marble and Alabaster 76
Medical 79
Metal 80
Miscellaneous 82
Music 95
Paintings and Pictures 97
Paper 102
Paperweights 107
Pens 110
Pewter 111
Photography 112
Plastic and Celluloid 114
Pottery and Porcelain 116
Purses 122
Rugs 123
Security 128
Silver 137
Textiles, Including Clothes 143
Tools 151
Tortoiseshell .152
Toys and Banks 153
Trunks 156
Wood 158
Words of Wisdom from Ralph and Terry 160
Product Sources 161
Index 163

Introduction

Your heirloom tea set is tarnishing on that wobbly table you found at a flea market. The dog chewed your wicker chair and the family photos are fading. The furniture needs polishing, the bottle collection would look great displayed in the window, and friends keep telling you to repaint your old metal toys. Here are 799 tips and value hints that will help with these and other concerns of living with collectibles, like how to use them and how to keep them in the best condition for posterity (or at least for your heirs). The tips tell you what to clean or restore, how to do it, how to display, protect, and enhance your collectibles.

This is not a book filled with serious, museum-approved instructions on how to restore furniture and other antiques. It is a household guide to sensible restoration and preservation. Tips include old-fashioned as well as quirky modern polishes, and remedies made from ingredients like ashes, ketchup, or false-teeth cleanser. Some suggestions will make you smile—after all, how many of us try to vacuum a moose head? All of the suggestions can be used by an amateur, or even an almost expert. Extensive repair or restoration should be done only by an expert in the field. So we also tell you what you should *not* try to do alone.

The book is divided into chapters from Advertising Collectibles to Wood. There is also a Miscellaneous chapter that includes tips such as what to do to limit earthquake damage to collections or how to pack for a move. And everyone should read the chapter about Security. It does no good to coddle your collection if burglars steal it.

Tucked between the tips are "value hints" that might lead to a great find at a flea market or sale. They even tell you what refinishing or restoration does to the resale price.

Sometimes at the end of a chapter there is a list of other chapters you should read. It is logical to look in the Advertising chapter for tips about care of signs, and tin signs are included. But restoration and care of *paper* signs is included in the Paper chapter.

We hope you enjoy our lighthearted look at a serious job. But our favorite is the lazy housekeeper's motto: "The less you dust, the less you polish, the less you handle the antiques you live with, the safer they will be."

KOVELS'
Quick Tips

Advertising Collectibles

SOME "COLLECTIONS" SHOULD BE TAKEN APART

❖ Advertising card collectors should be careful how the cards are displayed. Don't use the photo albums with plastic envelopes and a sticky cardboard backing (sometimes called "magnetic" albums). The cards will stick and the backs will be ruined. Pure pharmacy acetone, carefully dripped under the corner of the card, might help you remove it. Do not use nail polish remover. Don't use albums with black paper pages—they are too acid.

❖ Check the album to be sure there are no inked names or other wanted information that might wash off. Then, to remove trade cards from old white paper album pages, first try soaking the pages in a mixture of 2 gallons warm water and 1 cup white vinegar.

Or,

❖ If this fails, put the album in the freezer overnight, then drop into the vinegar water in the morning. If the glue is made of flour paste, the cards will come off, or can be carefully loosened in 20 minutes. Rinse the cards in clear warm water and rub off any remaining glue with a soft, wet towel.

☛ VALUE HINT

Any lithographed can with a picture is of more value to the collector than a lithographed can with just names. Any paper-labeled can that can be dated before 1875 is rare.

☛ VALUE HINT

Any ad that pictures an American flag or an African-American has added value. Known brand names are also of greater value.

WHERE TO HANG IT

❖ Tin signs and cans will fade from the ultraviolet rays coming in a sunny window or from a fluorescent light. Plexiglas UF-1 or UF-3 will cover the window and keep the rays away from your collection. There is also plastic film that cuts out the rays. Use protective plastic sleeves to cover fluorescent tubes.

❖ To hang an old Coca-Cola tray, use a wire plate holder but cover the bent parts that touch the tray with plastic tubing. Thin tubing is sold at pet stores for use in fish aquariums.

☛ VALUE HINT

Most Coca-Cola trays had green or brown borders in the 1920s, red borders in the 1930s.

☛ VALUE HINT

Billy Beer cans are not worth hundreds of dollars even though this myth appears in newspapers about every six months. Ads offer the cans for $1 to $3 each.

❖ A paper beer bottle label reacts to wet and dry the way hair does. If the label is curled, cover it with water to wet the fibers, then dry it flat.

❖ To "uncrush" a beer can, fill it up to the top with dried split peas. Just drop them in the hole, then add water to the top. Let stand and add water again an hour later. In about three hours the swelling peas will push all the dents from the can. Remove the peas or they may keep swelling and crack the can at a weak spot. This works only if the hole in the top is taped shut.

TINS

❖ Rusty tin may be helped. Rinse the metal, scrub, dry, then coat with a very thin layer of Vaseline.

❖ Remove rust from old tins and signs with OxySolv rust remover or a similar product. It is a degreaser rust remover used by auto garages and machine shops.

❖ To clean lithographed tin cans or signs, try using Saniwax and 0000-grade steel wool, but use with extreme caution. Too much rubbing will remove all of the design.

❖ Keep lithographed tins and signs out of sunlight. They will fade.

❖ If you have a smelly tin can, try filling it with fragrant peppermint tea for a few weeks. When you empty it, the tin will still smell, but like peppermint.

More good advice in the chapters about Dolls, Paper, Textiles, and Toys.

Aluminum

❖ Wash aluminum with mild dishwashing soap. Rinse and dry. If needed, use silver polish to add more luster. High temperatures in the dishwasher or oven will dull the shine.

❖ Fifties aluminum chairs and other brushed aluminum can be cleaned with a paste silver polish or a metal cleaner like Nevr-Dull.

☛ *VALUE HINT*

Most hammered aluminum dates from the 1930s. It is still being made. Look for pieces by Cellini Craft and Beunilum, and early pieces by Wendell August Forge.

More help may be found in the Metal chapter.

Animal Trophies

AFTER YOU SHOOT IT . . .

❖ Dust most trophies at least every other week. Dust and dirt damage the animal skin. Always dust from the head to the back, in the direction of the fur or feathers. Vacuum animals once every three years.

❖ Rub linseed oil on dull deer antlers, but use floor wax on African antelope or wild sheep horns.

❖ Never display a stuffed trophy in bright sunlight. Feathers and hair become stiff and brittle and colors fade.

❖ Never display a stuffed trophy over a fireplace. The heat will eventually dry the skin and injure the trophy.

❖ Insects like to eat all sorts of natural specimens. Mothballs and insect sprays will help keep stuffed animal heads free of moths or carpet beetles. Stuffed animals or birds should be mothproofed regularly.

❖ Clean the feathers on a stuffed bird with chunks of fresh white bread. After cleaning, spray lightly with hair spray.

❖ Never vacuum a bird. Feathers will fly. Wash gently with mild soap and water every five years.

❖ Always vacuum your moose from the snout up and scrub your pheasant with fresh white bread, torn not sliced. Vacuum your moose head with the furniture attachment but go with, not against, the grain. Rinse the head with water every five years. Careful—too much water will make a mildewed moose. After cleaning your stuffed moose head, polish the hair with a wad of nylon stocking.

Architectural

❖ A stained-glass window is probably more stable than it looks. Small cracks in the glass, even a bowed window, are usually not a problem. Cracked solder joints between pieces of glass should be repaired. If the window leaks air and presents a heating problem, build a storm window inside the stained glass.

❖ Never use commercial window cleaner on a stained-glass window. It could remove the color or damage the lead.

READY, SET, GO!

❖ Set your sundial at noon, June 15. Place it so the shadow falls on the 12. That's the only day when it is easy to set the sundial for the correct time. Adjust your thinking, not the sundial, for daylight saving time.

Baseball Cards

A CLEANUP LIST

❖ Don't trim cards to remove dirt or tears. It will lower the value.

❖ Dirty or warped cards should be wiped with a sponge dipped in a mild solution of detergent and water. The detergent will help make the cards cleaner and more pliable. Warped cards should be wiped, dried, then put under a heavy weight for a few days.

Check other care procedures in the Paper chapter.

Baskets

A TISKET, A TASKET . . .

❖ Do not moisten a rye straw basket. If it gets too wet, it may mold.

❖ Never oil a basket. It will attract dirt.

❖ Let your baskets share the bathroom with you when you take a shower. The hot, moist air is good for most baskets. Splint baskets should have an occasional light shower. Shake off the excess water. Dry the basket in a shady spot.

Books

❖ A library should be thoroughly cleaned at least once a year. Dirt attracts bugs and damages books. Always remove a book from the shelf to dust. All sides need cleaning.

❖ Don't pull an old book off the shelf by the spine. Don't pack books on the shelf so closely that it is a struggle to get a book out.

❖ To remove a musty odor from a book, sprinkle talcum powder between the pages, then wrap the book and store it for a few months. When you open it again, brush out all the powder and the musty smell will be gone.

Or, try this:

❖ The leather cover of a book should be wiped with a mixture of equal parts alcohol and water. The pages of the book should be warmed. Stand the book on edge, open it, and blow-dry it with a portable hair dryer on high heat.

❖ Leather-covered books and humans like the same humidity.

More easy-to-read tips in the Paper and Leather chapters.

Bottles

❖ When cleaning old bottles, save all labels and identifying tags.

❖ To remove a stubborn stain from the outside of a bottle, try this: Fill a bucket with soft sand. Push the bottle in and out of the sand, rotate it, and try to loosen the stain. Then wash in clean water.

❖ To remove a stain inside a bottle, put a handful of gravel in the bottle and shake vigorously.

Or,

❖ Clean the inside of a bottle with detergent powder and a Water Pik. The pressure from the Water Pik helps remove the stains.

Or,

❖ Polident or other false-teeth cleaners are good to use to remove scum from the inside of old glass bottles.

❖ To clean the residue out of an old perfume bottle, try this: Spray some window cleaner in the bottle, then rinse. If this fails, partially fill the bottle with nail polish remover and shake it. Wait about 15 minutes, empty, and rinse. It may help to poke at the residue with a shish kebab stick. Do not get any liquids on the label. Avoid harsh glass stain removers.

❖ If you want to clean a bottle that has a paper label, try to protect the label. Wrap the bottle tightly in thin plastic wrap. Seal the wrap with tape and rubber bands. Clean the inside carefully, using a mixture of water, automatic dishwasher detergent, and slightly abrasive cat litter. Fill bottle partway and shake.

❖ If a bottle stopper is stuck, first try using Liquid Wrench, an oil found at the hardware store, to loosen it.

Or,

❖ To remove a bottle stopper that is stuck, mix ½ teaspoon salt, 1 teaspoon rubbing alcohol, and ½ teaspoon glycerin. Pour the mixture around the stopper and let it seep in for a day. Then remove the stopper. If it's still stuck, try to encourage it by gently tapping the neck of the bottle with a wooden spoon. Some stoppers may be impossible to remove.

❖ To remove a dried cork that has fallen inside a bottle, try this: Pour some household ammonia in the bottle. Let it sit for a few days. Most of the cork should dissolve and can easily be removed.

❖ Don't use old home canning jars to preserve food. The jars with wire bails, glass caps, zinc porcelain-lined caps, or metal caps with rubber rings do not seal as well as the new two-piece vacuum-cap jars.

☞ *VALUE HINT—DATING*

A dating tip for bottle collectors: The words "Federal Law forbids sale or re-use of this bottle" were used on liquor bottles from 1933 to 1964. You can date an old bottle from the spelling of the word "Pittsburgh." From 1891 to 1911 the *h* was removed by the U.S. Board of Geographic names. The old spelling was resumed because of complaints from residents of Pittsburgh. Early bottles were blown or mold blown. In 1903, automatic bottling machines started to make bottles. You can tell from the seam on the side of the neck.

❖ To dry a small-necked bottle, give it a last rinse with alcohol or blow-dry with a hair dryer set to the coolest setting.

❖ Do not keep wine and spirits in lead crystal decanters. The lead will leach out and go into the wine. It is unhealthy to drink liquid that has absorbed lead.

❖ To make a quick "photo" of your old bottle for insurance records, try using a copying machine. Put the bottle on the machine, then cover it with white paper or cloth to block out any extra light. Lower the cover gently and take the picture.

More clear, concise information in the Glass chapter.

Brass

THAT BRASSY LOOK

❖ Brass that has been lacquered should be cleaned only with a solution of liquid dishwashing detergent and warm sudsy water, then rinsed in warm water and dried. Polish will harm the lacquer.

❖ Everyone seems to have a suggestion for cleaning brass. We recommend cleaning it with commercial brass polish. Wear white cotton gloves. The gloves make the difference.

❖ Others say brass can be polished with this homemade remedy: Make a paste of equal parts salt, flour, and vinegar. Rub the paste on the brass with a soft cloth. Rinse completely. Buff with a clean, dry, soft cloth.

Or, try this:

❖ Worcestershire sauce is a good brass polish.

❖ To clean intricate brass hardware, remove the hardware from the furniture. Keep track of the screws and return them to the exact same holes. Soak the hardware in a solution of equal parts lemon juice and water for about a half hour. Brush with an old toothbrush. Rinse and wipe dry. Rub paste wax on the brass.

❖ Don't overclean hardware, andirons, or other old brass objects. Clean off the worst, but don't try to make them look brand-new.

❖ Never polish Trench Art pieces made of brass shell casings. Collectors prefer the dark-colored metal.

❖ After polishing brass kept outdoors, use a thin coat of paste wax to protect the shine.

☞ *VALUE HINT*

A magnet will not be attracted to solid brass. It *will* cling to brass-plated iron.

Turn to the Bronze and Metal chapters for more suggestions.

Bronze

KEEP THE BEAUTY OF BRONZE

❖ Don't use bleaching cleansing powders or disinfectant floor-washing products that contain chlorine in a room that has bronze figures on display. Chlorine harms bronzes.

❖ Be careful when cleaning bronze figurines, lamp bases, bowls, etc. Never use steel wool, stiff brushes, or chemicals. They will remove the surface patina and lower the value. Never wash a bronze. Never use metal polish on a bronze. Dust frequently.

❖ Scratches on bronze cannot be polished off without destroying the patina and lowering the value.

☞ *VALUE HINT*

If you buy an Art Deco bronze-and-ivory figure, be very careful to examine the ivory. Even slight cracks or damage lowers the value. Reproductions often use plastic instead of ivory.

❖ Outdoor bronze sculptures need special care. Wash with soap, water, and a little ammonia to remove oil and dirt. Then rinse, dry, and rub with a cloth dipped in olive oil or boiled linseed oil. Rub with a dry cloth to remove extra oil. Outdoor bronzes should be oiled or waxed several times a year.

You might find more help in the chapter on Metal.

Candlesticks and Candles

HOT PROBLEM

❖ Candle drippings can be removed from fabric or furniture with the help of ice cubes. Rub the wax with the ice until the wax hardens. Scrape off the hard wax with a credit card or stiff cardboard. If some wax remains, put a blotter over it, then iron with a cool iron.

❖ Candlesticks will melt or even explode if candles burn too low. Be extra careful when burning candles in glass candlesticks. If the candle burns too low, the hot wax and flame may crack the glass. Always support the arm of a candelabrum when putting in the candles.

❖ To easily remove wax that has dripped on a candlestick, put the candlestick in the freezer for about an hour. The wax will flake off. Sometimes you can melt the wax off with very hot water, but don't do this with wooden or painted candlesticks.

❖ To clean wax from glass candlesticks, scrape with a wooden stick, then wash off the remaining wax with rubbing alcohol.

Enlightening tips for care of candlesticks are also found in the Glass, Pottery, and Silver chapters.

Carousels

ROUND AND ROUND

❖ Some collectors want carousel horses that have been completely restored. Some buy only pieces with original paint. This is one type of collectible that can be restored without a loss in value. The work should be done by an expert. This rule is true for a few other types of painted wooden folk art, too.

☛ *VALUE HINTS*

American carousel figures are more heavily carved on the right side because they went around counterclockwise. The left side is more ornate for European carousel figures because the carousel turned the other way. American figures sell for more money.

Old, authentic carousel figures almost always have glass eyes or realistic horse-shaped eyes. Reproductions have human-shaped eyes, either Asian or Caucasian. Beware: there are many fakes.

Carousel figures are usually made of wood and need the same care as furniture. Check the Furniture chapter and the Wood chapter.

Cartoons and Animation Cels

NOT A JOKE TO CARE FOR

❖ The paintings on celluloid called "cels" should be kept away from direct sunlight and high humidity. They should be framed with acid-free mats. Be sure the picture does not touch the glass.

☛ *VALUE HINT*

Date Mickey Mouse from his appearance. He has changed in the 60 years since his introduction in *Steamboat Willie*. Originally, he didn't have pupils in his eyes. His legs were like pipe cleaners, now they have shape. He had a neck and white inside his ears in his middle years, but none when young or old. His nose has gotten shorter and more tilted.

For more information on the best way to frame and display a cel, look for tips in the Miscellaneous, Paintings, and Paper chapters. Comic books and comic strips are made of paper, so check the Paper chapter. Toys are in the chapter on toys.

Chrome

CHASE AWAY THE DIRT

❖ Old newspapers can be used to polish water spots off chrome.

❖ Use commercial chrome polish (sold for automobile chrome) to clean your old chrome bowls and pitchers and remove small scratches.

Since chrome is metal, you may find more information in the Metal chapter.

Clocks

TIME TO CLEAN AND FIX

☞ *VALUE HINT*

If you find a clock with a complete, original paper label, add 35 percent to the value.

❖ Never wind an old clock counterclockwise. But—think twice about this—clocks that are wound from the back should be wound counterclockwise because that is really clockwise from the front of the clock.

❖ To set the time, push the minute hand clockwise, never counterclockwise. If the clock chimes, be sure to wait until it stops striking before you advance the hands again or the clock will hit the wrong number of strikes. If that happens, wind it without waiting for strikes until everything is back in sync.

❖ Wind the clock fully each time you wind it.

❖ Clocks should be cleaned and lubricated every five years.

❖ Clean a clock face as seldom as possible. The brass trim may be coated with colored lacquer and brass polish will remove the color.

A damaged porcelain clock face is difficult to repair. It will lower the price of a clock by 20 to 30 percent.

❖ A dental mirror is useful when checking for damage or repairs inside a clock.

☞ VALUE HINT

Fakers sometimes "marry" a clock works and a clock case. Examine a clock carefully to be sure the parts are all original.

❖ Be sure to remove the weights and pendulum when moving a grandfather clock. Check carefully to be sure it is still level and prop the base if necessary. A clock that is off-level will not keep accurate time. Remove the pendulum if possible when moving a shelf clock.

❖ Be sure your grandfather clock is on a level floor and move it as little as possible. To make the clock run faster, raise the pendulum; to slow it, lower the pendulum.

❖ Put about 15 inches of plastic "popcorn" in the bottom of your tall case clock cabinet. The weights sometimes fall, damaging the bottom boards, so this will solve the problem before it happens.

❖ Don't set up a grandfather clock near a heat register or radiator.

❖ Ebonized clocks should be cleaned once a year with paste wax.

❖ Cuckoo clocks sometimes need minor first aid or major repair. First try home remedies. If the clock stops, it may be because it is not level. Try shifting the clock a bit. The clock will not run correctly in a draft. Hang it so it is flat against the wall. Major repairs should be done by a professional.

❖ Attach your grandfather clock to the wall if it seems the least bit unsteady.

Clock case care tips can be found in the Furniture, Marble, and Wood chapters.

Collector Plates and Figurines

USE UNLIMITED CARE

❖ If you use plate hangers to display your plates, be sure they are not too tight. The clips should be covered with a soft material. Otherwise the end clips may scratch or chip the plate. Put a piece of cardboard between the back of the plate and the wire plate holder to protect the back from scratching.

❖ Hummel figurines should be cleaned by washing in liquid detergent and water, half and half. Never put them in the dishwasher.

☛ *VALUE HINTS*

Never throw out the plate's original box or papers. They add to the resale value.

Your homeowner's insurance probably doesn't cover the full value of your limited edition plates or figurines. You will need a fine arts policy with a breakage clause.

Follow the other rules found in the Pottery chapter.

Copper

PENNY BRIGHT

❖ Don't cook acid foods in copper pots unless they have a tin lining. The combination of acid and copper creates a poison.

❖ Polish copper, brass, or pewter only once or twice a year.

❖ Try the old-time recipe for cleaning copper. Mix lemon juice or vinegar with salt and use as a metal polish.

❖ Ketchup is a good emergency copper cleaner.

❖ To hang copper molds in your kitchen, try this method: Mount a solid brass or wooden curtain rod across the top of the hanging area. Molds can then be hung by hooks and easily moved when new ones are added.

❖ Do not try to clean copper with an original patinated finish like Heintz Art, Gorham, or Tiffany. Removing the dark finish lowers the value.

More tips in the Metal chapter.

Dolls

☛ *VALUE HINT*

Save your doll's packaging, tags, and inserts. These can triple the price when the doll is sold.

CLEANING AND STORING

❖ When storing dolls, old or new, be sure to remove any sticky tape that might have been used to hold bows, etc., in place. The glue from the tape will eventually discolor the fabric. If dolls are to be stored a long time, put tissue between clothing and doll to keep bright colors from "bleeding" onto the doll. Remove metal that might rust. Save the box and all tags.

❖ Dolls with inset eyes should be stored face down.

❖ Check your dolls regularly to be sure no insects have moved into the sawdust filling or tasty wool fabrics.

❖ If your doll's body leaks sawdust, try patching the hole by putting a few drops of clear glue in the hole. If the hole is too large, patch it with a piece of muslin or kid cut from an old glove. Cut a circular patch and glue in place.

❖ To clean sleep eyes on a doll, fill an eye dropper with iso-propyl alcohol diluted by half with water. Put the doll on its back and hold the eyes open. Drop the solution into each eye, adding liquid until the eyeball is covered. Open and close the eyelid several times. Turn the doll face down and let the fluid drain out. Then stand the doll upright, hold a clean cloth against the eyes, and tip the doll until the last of the liquid drains out.

❖ After you clean your doll, wipe it with a cloth dipped in distilled water. Soap residue will cause discoloration.

❖ Don't wash, set, comb, or change the original hair on a doll. It lowers the value.

❖ Don't wash your doll's dresses. Keep them mint.

WOODEN DOLLS WOULDN'T MIND

❖ If wooden nesting dolls stick, try putting a few drops of baby oil into the space between the dolls. Then try separating the dolls. This may stain unpainted surfaces, so be careful. Wipe off all oil immediately.

❖ Check wooden dolls for insect damage and infestation. Isolate the doll until you have chemically treated it to remove the insects.

❖ Never wash a wooden doll if you can avoid it. If there is no other way to remove the dirt, be sure to wet the cloth and then clean the doll. Don't wet the doll.

CLEAN CLOTH DOLLS CAREFULLY

❖ If you buy an old cloth doll, put it in a closed box with an insect strip for 48 hours to be sure there are no insects. Be sure the strip does not touch the doll.

❖ To clean a cloth doll, first vacuum through a layer of nylon net. Don't vacuum silk.

❖ Don't clean a cloth doll's body with water; use cornstarch or talc. Rub it into the fabric, then gently brush it away after four hours.

☛ *VALUE HINT*

If you bought a Cabbage Patch doll as an investment, it is best to keep it mint in the box. Save all papers, correspondence, and even newspaper clippings telling about the 1983 Christmas season sellouts.

❖ Felt dolls are difficult to clean. Swirl them in cornstarch, then leave them in it for a day or two. Brushing may help.

❖ Vinyl dolls should not be stored in a hot attic. Heat may darken the vinyl.

❖ If you have a vinyl doll with dirt or pencil marks on the head or body, try this: Wrap the doll so that only the marked part shows. Rub the mark with solid vegetable shortening and put the doll in the sun for the day. Try this for several days and the mark should disappear. Soft vinyl dolls, popular in the 1950s, often are stained with green, blue, or black marks. These are probably from mold, not from ink or paints. Buy a commercial mold and mildew remover that is chlorine-free. Test it in an inconspicuous spot, then wipe it on the entire doll. Wash with warm soapy water, rinse, and dry. Any remaining stain can be bleached.

❖ Hard plastic dolls will mildew if kept in a damp environment. Remove mildew and mold stains from dolls with a commercial, chlorine-free bathroom shower cleaning product.

❖ Be sure your doll clothes have not been washed with a chlorine-based product like bleach. The chemical reaction will eventually destroy the plastic "skin" of the doll.

BARBIE'S BEAUTY PROBLEMS

❖ To clean a Barbie doll's arms and legs, use a cotton swab soaked in acetone. Do not use on the vinyl body or face. Clean these with rubbing alcohol.

❖ The 1961 Brownette Barbie often has a greasy face. An ingredient used in the vinyl is slowly being rejected and a greasy film appears on the face while the head slowly shrinks. Remove the head. Wipe it inside and out with alcohol, then fill the head with baking soda. It will soak up any future grease. Return the filled head to the doll. You may want to have this done at a doll hospital.

❖ Green ears are a problem for Barbie dolls. The green is a reaction between the vinyl head and the metal posts that hold the earrings. Remove Barbie's head. Put Clearasil maximum-strength vanishing lotion or Tarnex silver polish on a piece of cotton and place the cotton on each ear. Put the Barbie's head in a covered dish and ignore it for four days. The stain should be bleached out.

You might get more help in the Toys chapter.

Furniture

DON'T FOOL AROUND WITH THE FINISH ON FINE FURNITURE

❖ We had a friend whose pet cougar liked to chew on the legs of her 18th-century American chairs. Not good for the chairs! Don't even let your dogs or cats near valuable old furniture.

☛ *VALUE HINTS*

Serious collecting of antique furniture began in the 1920s. Fakers began to make great pieces from average pieces. Butterfly tables were made from tavern tables, block-front bureaus from plain bureaus; inlaid eagles and other designs were added to furniture and clocks. Plain highboys were "improved" with scroll tops. Plain legs of tea tables were carved. A faker often carves an extra design on the lid of a desk. Birdcage supports and piecrust edges were added to plain tables. Altered pieces have very low values.

Examine a piece of furniture and look for unexplained holes, stains, and fade marks. They may indicate a fake.

Fakers sometimes make a round table with leaves from a square table with leaves because it would have more value. This can be spotted if you carefully examine the overall proportion of the table and the edges of the top.

❖ Be sure the big furniture you buy is small enough to go through the door into your room.

❖ Don't ship furniture to a place that is noticeably hotter or colder, or wetter or drier, if it can be avoided. The wood will expand or contract, causing cracks and other damage.

❖ Never pick a chair up by the arms. Pick it up under the seat. The arms could loosen or crack.

❖ Always remove the top drawers from a large chest first. If you pull out the bottom drawers and then move the chest, it is likely to tip over.

❖ Never push antique furniture across the floor. Pick it up. Old furniture may have weak glue joints and the feet may pop off.

❖ Try to rearrange your furniture once a year to avoid noticeable sun-fading of wood and fabrics.

❖ Rearrange lamps, figurines, vases, and other knickknacks on tabletops. If you don't, the exposed wood will be lighter than the covered sections under the ornaments.

❖ Glue weather stripping to the bottom of a chair rocker to protect the floor or carpet.

❖ When moving furniture, always tie drawers and doors in place. Use soft cloth tape.

THE LESS YOU DO, THE BETTER IT IS FOR THE FURNITURE

❖ Treat your furniture the same way you treat your face. Wash it to remove the dirt. You do not want to remove the skin. Don't sand too much or use a "dip strip."

❖ Put a little furniture polish on a damp cloth when you dust wooden furniture. You won't have to polish as often.

❖ Experts say you should keep your furniture clean and dust-free, wax it twice a year with paste wax, and not let it dry out.

❖ Infrequent waxing of furniture is best. We always knew lazy housekeeping with antiques was the best. Do as little as possible to clean and shine pieces and avoid creating problems.

❖ To get a good shine on your antique furniture, use more rubbing, not more polish.

☛ *VALUE HINT*

If you see any numbers or letters on the frame of a wooden piece of furniture, do not remove or erase them. They may refer to a catalog, and eventually you may be able to attribute the piece to the proper manufacturer, thus adding value.

❖ Different types of furniture polish give different finishes. Liquid, oil polish, and paste wax leave a high luster. Cream polish and spray wax leave a medium luster.

❖ Use one type of furniture polish. If you switch from an oil to a wax polish, the surface will appear smudged.

❖ Never use spray polish on antique furniture. It will leave a gray haze and attracts dirt. It is not safe to put spray wax over paste wax because it may soften the paste wax and spoil the finish.

❖ No commercial furniture polish will damage the finish of furniture, but avoid silicone-based brands. Eventually the polish will wear off or be wiped off. Some homemade remedies are damaging, however. Do not use boiled linseed oil mixtures.

❖ For a safe, pollution-free furniture cleaner, use a mixture of 1 cup olive or vegetable oil and ½ cup lemon juice.

❖ When waxing intricately carved furniture, apply the paste wax with a stenciling brush. Use a shoe brush to buff the wax.

❖ Old pantyhose are good to use to put an oil finish on furniture. Remove all elastic first. The material doesn't leave lint.

☛ *VALUE HINT*

Refinished Mission furniture is worth 10 to 25 percent less than furniture with the original finish.

HOME ENVIRONMENT IS IMPORTANT

❖ Don't ignore signs of "wildlife." Use sprays and exterminators. Moths and carpet beetles eat upholstery and fabrics; termites eat wood; powder post beetles and dry wood termites eat wood.

❖ You can't win! Homes in cold areas with central heating must be humidified to keep the furniture from drying and cracking. Homes in warm areas must be *de*humidified to keep condensation from rotting the wood.

THOSE UNWANTED RINGS

❖ Wood-boring beetle larvae sometimes find their way into furniture in a house. The adult beetles emerge in July or August and fly to other pieces of furniture. Watch for signs of pinhead-sized holes or sawdust. Then spray immediately and treat with the appropriate bug-killing chemicals.

❖ A white ring on a tabletop is in the finish, a black ring is in the wood. It is easier to remove a damaged finish than a wood stain. To remove white rings—usually made by damp glasses or hot cups of coffee—from wooden tabletops, rub the spot with a mixture of mayonnaise and toothpaste. Wipe, then polish.

Or,

❖ To remove white rings, use paste wax and 0000-grade steel wool. Rub with the grain. Buff with a wad of cheese-cloth.

Or,

❖ White rings can sometimes be removed with liquid metal polish or auto paint cleaner. Apply the cleaner to a soft cloth and rub until the ring is gone. Then repolish the surface with furniture polish.

Or,

❖ Try rubbing in a little cigar ash to open the finish lightly. If this doesn't work, thoroughly rub in a nondrying oil such as lemon or almond oil. Follow with a regular wax paste.

Out, out, d——spots

❖ Watch out for water spills from a floral centerpiece.

❖ White water spots on tabletops can be a problem. Mix 2 tablespoons white vinegar in 1 pint mineral oil. Rub on the tabletop. Test a small spot before starting, because a few finishes may not accept this mixture.

Or,

❖ Try this method to remove white water spots from wood: Put a piece of blotter paper over the spot and press with a warm iron. The spot should vanish. If it does not, rub it with lemon oil.

Cover the stains and scratches

❖ To cover a scratch in a piece of furniture made of dark wood, rub a walnut, Brazil nut, or butternut into the scratch. Eyebrow pencil or shoe polish in a matching shade will also work.

❖ Slightly scratched or damaged wooden furniture will look much better if it is waxed with a high-quality paste wax. Don't use spray or liquid wax because it has other added chemicals that may cause problems. Apply the wax with a tightly woven soft cotton cloth, not cheesecloth because it may snag. Wax only once a year. Buff monthly.

❖ Scratches on plastic furniture can be hidden with regular applications of automobile wax.

❖ A brisk rubbing with olive oil will remove most alcohol stains from wood.

❖ Brown shoe polish is good to cover scuffs and slight damage on furniture. Cover scratches on dark cherry or mahogany by rubbing them with a bit of cotton dipped in iodine. Scratches on lighter woods can be covered by using a piece of cotton dipped in a solution of equal parts iodine and alcohol.

❖ Cigarette burns on wooden furniture are hard to conceal. Rub the burn with scratch-cover polish. If that doesn't help, rub the burn with a paste of rottenstone (found in most hardware stores) and linseed oil.

❖ Buy a paint-by-number kit to get an inexpensive assortment of paint colors to use for touch-ups and restorations for furniture.

❖ A fresh ink stain on wood can be removed by washing with water and then applying lemon juice.

❖ Fresh bloodstains can be removed from wood with a rag soaked in hydrogen peroxide.

❖ For a quick, new finish on inexpensive furniture, try this: Rub colored furniture wax on old wooden pieces, let dry for 15 minutes to eight hours, then buff with a terry cloth rag. Wait a few days, then apply clear furniture wax and buff. Be sure the colored wax is just slightly darker than the original wood finish.

❖ If you have an old wooden table of little value, you might want to try adding color with Rit dye. The color can never be removed, so don't use this on any good antiques.

STUCK?

❖ Have you ever pulled a drawer handle and had it fall off the drawer? This is not uncommon for very old furniture with bail handles. The best way to get the handleless drawer open is to use a plunger, the plumber's friend. Stick it to the front of the drawer, then pull.

❖ A drawer that is stuck can be helped by heat, which will shrink the wood. Remove any nearby drawers, then aim a hair dryer set on medium at the drawer. Concentrate on the spot that seems stuck. Once the drawer is opened, rub the runners with soap or a candle.

❖ Never wash lacquered wood. Just wipe it clean with a damp cloth. Water could seep into the base wood and cause damage.

CARE FOR EXOTIC FINISHES

❖ Very dirty lacquer can be cleaned with a paste of flour and olive oil.

❖ When cleaning mother-of-pearl inlay, use a weak solution of detergent, never an acid. A Q-Tip will help. Try not to touch the areas near the inlay.

❖ If you spill nail polish on furniture, try this cure: Rub the spot with 0000-grade steel wool dipped in liquid wax polish. Wipe, then rewax with your usual furniture polish.

❖ If a piece of paper is stuck to the finish of a dresser top, try this: Soak the paper with mineral oil. Let it sit a few hours, then rub with a rough cloth. Repeat until the paper is removed. Don't use sandpaper or scouring pads.

❖ Felt tops on card tables and desks attract moths. Vacuum tops carefully at least once a year.

If you are concerned about a clock, you will find more tips in the Clocks chapter.

WICKER CARE

❖ If you own a wicker chair that makes small popping noises when you sit in it, dampen it with water. It is too dry, and wicker may crack if not kept moist.

❖ If you keep wicker furniture inside, be sure to have a humidifier or lots of plants nearby.

❖ Wrapped wicker furniture should be repaired as soon as possible. Rewrap the wicker and glue the end with white glue.

❖ If your wicker furniture is very dusty, take it to the gas station and blow the dust away with the air hose.

☞ *VALUE HINT*

Date wicker furniture from the label. Wakefield Rattan Co. was used from 1855 to 1897; Heywood-Wakefield Co., 1868–1897; Heywood Bros. & Wakefield Co., 1897–1921; Heywood-Wakefield Co., after 1921.

SMELLY STUFF

❖ Mildew, fungus, stains, and odors can be removed from the wooden parts of furniture by using a commercial mildew remover found at the supermarket. Wipe the entire piece or it will have a lighter spot where it was cleaned.

❖ Remove the musty smell from a bureau drawer, trunk, cupboard, or box by sprinkling fresh ground coffee inside. Leave it for 24 hours.

Or,

❖ Sprinkle the inside with baking soda and leave it there for a week. Vacuum. Repeat if necessary. If the smell is from an animal, try washing the wood with a solution of neutroleum alpha, found in pet stores.

Or,

❖ Parch several handfuls of uncooked rice in a shallow pan in the oven. Then put the pan and rice in the musty drawer. You may have to repeat the parching to keep the moisture and mildew from reappearing.

Or,

❖ Try spreading cat litter on the inside. Close the drawer or lid for several days. Repeat until the odor seems gone. Then wash the inside and let it dry.

Or,

❖ Put the piece outside in the shade. Plug in a fan and blow air through the drawers and frame. If that does not work after several days, fill the drawers with baking soda, cat litter, or charcoal chips that may absorb the odor.

KEEP THE "LOOK"

❖ Large mirrors should not be taken down to be cleaned. Get an assistant to hold the mirror steady while it is being wiped.

❖ Use an old nylon stocking bunched into a ball to clean a rough-surfaced mirror frame, carved wooden piece, or other irregular surface.

Early mirrors, those made before 1850, had thin glass. To judge the thickness of a mirror, hold a pencil point against the glass. The difference between the point and the reflection is the thickness. Early mirrors reflect a darker image than new mirrors.

❖ Scratches can be rubbed off the glass in a mirror by using a piece of felt and polishing rouge from a paint store.

❖ Gilt frames can be cleaned with beer.

KEEP IT GOLDEN

❖ Liquid household cleaner on a paper towel is a good way to clean gilding.

❖ Never use metal polish to clean ormolu or gilded metal parts. Polish will remove the top layer of color. Use ammonia.

❖ To clean a gold leaf frame, rub the gold leaf with a cloth that has been dipped in onion juice.

❖ Don't retouch gold leaf picture frames or other gold trim with anything but real gold leaf.

❖ Don't use gummed labels on colored paint or gilding on picture frames or furniture.

❖ Never buy a repainted chair if you can buy one with original paint. Never strip all the paint from a chair if you can restore the original paint. Repainting a chair lowers the value.

❖ Don't lock furniture with antique locks. If they stick, it is almost impossible to open the door or drawer without damaging the wood.

❖ If you want to use a lock on old furniture, be sure it is cleaned and oiled.

❖ Have an extra key made to fit doors and drawers in old furniture. Stick it to the bottom of the piece with a wad of gum or tape.

☞ *VALUE HINT*

> When buying a table, study the bottom. Look underneath the top and see if the legs are original, if the top seems to be in one piece, and if there are any unexpected screw or nail holes that indicate changes in the use of the wood.

❖ Nuts and bolts on old furniture hardware should be removed carefully. Wrap pliers with masking tape to protect the brass. Old brass is often soft.

❖ When removing a lock on an old piece of furniture, make a diagram of the lock. Tape each screw on the proper place on the diagram so you can return each one to its original hole. Old screws may be different lengths and putting a long screw in a short hole could cause damage.

❖ Rusty old lock in a drawer? Brush off the rust with a metal brush, then oil the lock. Test it before using it.

❖ Some old locks must have the key turned twice to open.

❖ When repairing furniture, reuse the old, original hardware nails. Keep track of nails as they are removed, so each will be returned to the same hole. Often they are different sizes.

❖ When replacing lost hardware with matching new pieces, put the new handles on the lowest drawers. The difference in patina will be less visible.

☛ *VALUE HINT*

Look at the hinge on a tilt-top table. The wear should show on both the top and the base if it is old.

❖ If the screw holding a hinge is loose, try this old-fashioned remedy. Break the heads off several large wooden kitchen matches. Put the wooden strips in the hole with some glue, then screw the old screw back into place.

STICK IT UP

❖ When repairing furniture, it is best to reglue before you refinish.

❖ When regluing loose rungs or parts of chairs, remove old glue with vinegar. Drip it into any holes with a small oil can.

❖ A rolltop on a rolltop desk can be repaired with window-shade material. Glue the slats to the material with white glue. Be careful; this is not an easy repair and slats must be spaced properly.

❖ If the veneer on old furniture is just loose, use a razor blade to make a small slit in the wood with the grain of the wood. Use this as a way to apply the glue under the veneer.

If the veneer is bubbled up and loose, place a piece of cardboard on the wood and press with an iron set at medium heat. The heat should soften the glue and you will be able to feel the wood give a little. Press down and weight the spot until the glue has redried.

❖ If you accidentally dust off a bit of veneer, a loose screw, or a piece of metal mounting, immediately put it in an envelope and put it in a drawer or tape or pin it to the back of the furniture. When you have time, decide if you or an expert should do the needed restoration. These small pieces should be carefully saved because they can never be exactly duplicated.

❖ If you reupholster an antique piece of furniture, save some of the original fabric. Put it in an envelope and tape it to the bottom of the seat so future owners can know more about the original appearance. When selling a piece, this sort of history will add to the value.

Lacquer is in its own chapter. So are Leather and Marble.

Games

KEEP THEM IN THE DARK

❖ Bright sunlight fades colors of game board boxes.

❖ We hung a 1950s Li'l Abner game board on the wall near a window. The sun removed all of the yellow color in a year. The grass in the print is now blue. The printed boards from the 1940s–1960s fade very quickly. Older printing seems to be less damaged by ultraviolet exposure.

☛ *VALUE HINTS*

Be sure all of the parts of a game are included in the box when you buy a game. Look at the condition of the box, the board, the cards, the spinner, and other small parts.

The only way to be sure no pieces are missing from a jigsaw puzzle is to put it together.

The Paper and Toys chapters may play a part in your care of games.

Glass

IT'S CLEAR HOW TO DO IT

❖ Antique glass should be handled as if it has been repaired and might fall apart. Hold a pitcher by the body, not the handle. Pick up stemware by holding both the stem and the bowl. Hold plates in two hands, not by the rim.

❖ Glassware, old or new, requires careful handling. Stand each piece upright, not touching another. Never nest pieces. Wash in moderately hot water and mild detergent. Avoid wiping gold- or platinum-banded pieces while glasses are hot. Never use scouring pads or silver polish on glass. When using an automatic dishwasher, be sure the water temperature is under 180 degrees.

❖ Glass plates that are cloudy may clean with silver polish and a plastic scouring pad. If the problem is a stain, it might clean. If it is damage from small scratches, it might look better for display if it is coated with a nonyellowing floor wax and then lightly buffed.

☛ *VALUE HINT*

To test the age of engraving on a glass tumbler or goblet, place a white handkerchief on the inside. If the engraving is old, the lines will usually show up darker than the rest of the glass. New engraving has a bright, powderlike surface. Old glass is usually much more valuable.

❖ Never put anything hot in a cut-glass bowl. It was not made to withstand heat and will crack.

❖ Never stack cut-glass bowls.

☛ *VALUE HINTS*

A signature adds 25 percent to the value of cut glass. Look carefully. Signatures are very faint.

The early 1840s were the time of pressed-glass table settings. Early patterns were simple, with heavy loops or ribbed effects. The 1870s brought more elaborate naturalistic patterns. Clear and frosted patterns with figures were in style during the 1870s. Overall patterns that were slightly geometric in feeling were in style by 1880, and patterns such as Daisy and Button and Hobnail came into vogue. Colored pressed-glass patterns became popular after the Civil War.

❖ A ground-glass perfume bottle stopper should be turned gently to the right for a snug fit. To remove the stopper, first turn it to the left to "unlock it" before pulling it out.

Tops for American glass cruets are almost always cut or pressed, not blown. Collectors pay more for American pieces.

❖ If two tumblers get stuck when stacked, try putting cold water into the inside glass, then put both into hot water up to the lower rim.

❖ Don't store foods or beverages in crystal bowls or bottles for long periods of time. Acidic juice, vinegar, and alcoholic beverages will leach out the lead in the glass. It is unhealthy to drink the liquid.

❖ Do not use gold- or silver-decorated glasses if the trim has turned chalky gray. This is a source of lead poisoning.

❖ Put a silver spoon in a glass before pouring in hot water. It will absorb heat and keep the glass from cracking.

❖ Spray the inside of a glass flower vase with a nonstick product made to keep food from sticking to cooking pots. This will keep the vase from staining if water is left in too long.

❖ Never allow water to evaporate in a glass vase. It will leave a white residue that may be impossible to remove.

❖ If you collect the decorated glasses from fast food restaurants, never wash them in the dishwasher. The heat and detergent will change the coloring and lower the value.

❖ Decorated glasses given as promotions at fast food restaurants often fade in sunlight.

CLEANING

❖ Be careful about putting antique glass in the dishwasher. Glass will sometimes crack from the heat.

❖ Put a rubber collar on the faucet spout over the sink and a rubber mat or towel on the bottom of the inside of the sink. This may save you from breaking glass or china you are washing.

❖ Never put hot glass in cold water, or cold glass in hot water. The temperature change can crack the glass.

☛ *VALUE HINT*

Custard glass and milk glass can now be repaired by black-light proof methods. Be very careful when buying old pieces.

❖ The best cleaner for your cut glass is a perfume-free, softener-free dishwashing detergent. Ammonia is too strong, and scented softeners sometimes leave an oily film.

❖ For a pollution-free glass cleaner, use a mixture of white vinegar and water.

❖ Don't use ammonia on glasses with gold or silver decorations.

❖ Do not wash or rinse gold-decorated glass with very hot water or strong soap. It will remove some of the gold.

❖ A glass vase or bowl can be cleaned with a damp cloth. Try not to put valuable old glass in a sink filled with water. Hitting the glass on a faucet or the sink is a common cause of breakage.

❖ If you have a small-neck decanter or bottle that doesn't seem to dry after it is washed, try putting a small amount of rubbing alcohol in the bottle. Shake, pour out, and wait for the remaining drops to evaporate.

❖ Wipe glass dry with newspapers for a special shine.

❖ Tired of scrubbing and scrubbing glass to remove marks from masking tape and labels? Get some commercial hand cleaner, pat some on the stain, let it stay for 30 minutes. Then rub it off with a cloth and wash the glass.

Or,

❖ To remove the remains of masking tape and labels from glass, rub the spot with WD-40 lubricating and penetrating oil.

❖ Having trouble with stain in a glass bottle or vase? Sometimes this type of stain can be removed. Fill the bottle with water, drop in an Alka-Seltzer, and let it soak for about 24 hours. Then rub the ring with a brush or a cloth.

If the deposit is a chemical deposit, this treatment should remove it. If the ring is actually caused by etching of the glass, it cannot be removed unless the bottle is polished.

❖ To remove the brown deposits found in old vinegar cruets, fill the cruets with diluted ammonia for a few hours, then rinse.

☛ *VALUE HINT*

Old milk glass is slightly opalescent at the edge when held up to a strong light. New glass is not.

❖ To clean carnival glass, try using a mixture of $\frac{1}{2}$ cup ammonia and $\frac{1}{8}$ cup white vinegar.

❖ Shallow nicks and rough edges on glass can sometimes be smoothed off with fine emery paper.

❖ To ship small pieces of glass, try this trick: Put the glass in a Styrofoam cup, then wrap in bubble wrap or several layers of paper. Stuff sides and bottom of a large box with Styrofoam trays. Then put the antiques on the trays. Pack more Styrofoam around them. Maybe you can get extra trays at your grocery store.

❖ If you move glass in cold weather, be sure to let it sit at room temperature for several hours before you try unpacking it. The glass will break more easily if there is an abrupt temperature change.

More tips for packing in the Miscellaneous chapter.

Graniteware

❖ Graniteware and other enameled kitchenwares should be cleaned with water and baking soda. If necessary, use chlorine bleach.

❖ Clean the inside of a graniteware pot by filling it with water and boiling peeled potatoes in it.

☞ *VALUE HINT*

Graniteware pieces made in the 1950s were lighter in weight and brighter in color than early 19th-century wares. The finish is smoother on old pieces. Most 1930s and after teapots and coffeepots had hinged lids and the handles were attached very close to the tops of the pots.

More help in Kitchen.

COLLECTIBLES DON'T TAKE A HOLIDAY

❖ Use your antiques on the holiday table, but be careful. Wax from candles can stain a cloth. Cranberry or other fruits can permanently stain dishes. Vases and plants often leak and make rings on the wood. Be sure to use a coaster or dish. Sap from the stems of greens draped on pictures or marble can stain. Most adhesives and transparent tape will leave a mark.

❖ Be careful where you put a fresh pumpkin or gourd at Halloween or Thanksgiving. Put a plastic liner underneath them. A rotting pumpkin will permanently stain wood or marble.

❖ Old papier-mâché jack-o'-lanterns originally had a thin piece of paper in the eyes. The light from the candle showed through the paper. You can make a replacement with tracing paper and watercolor paint.

CHRISTMAS ORNAMENTS

❖ Don't try to restore old ornaments. A little damage and wear adds to the charm of old Christmas ornaments. It indicates an antique that has seen many holidays of use. Restoration lowers value.

❖ Don't store glass ornaments in a damp basement. Mildew will cause damage.

❖ If you are a collector of old Christmas tree ornaments or Christmas lights, use them on the tree. Old electric lights should be checked before they are used. Do not use burning candles—it's too dangerous.

❖ Save the cap and hook from a broken ornament. The old ones will fit on other old ornaments and reproduction ornaments and look very different from shiny new caps.

Iron

❖ Remove the rust from iron by soaking the piece in kerosene for 24 hours, or use any commercial preparation made for the removal of rust. Then wash, dry, and coat the clean piece with a light oil to protect it.

❖ To clean small pieces of iron, try soaking them in white vinegar for 24 to 48 hours.

❖ Small nicks and scratches in decorative ironware can be covered with black crayon. Wipe off the excess with paper. Don't do this on pots and pans you may use for cooking.

❖ Old, used iron andirons are tarnished and covered with resin from the smoke. They should be cleaned with liquid metal polish and 0000-grade steel wool. Do not coat the clean andirons. The hot fire will eventually scorch any coating.

❖ Old heating grates of iron have a new use. Put them on the outdoor mat to be used as mud scrapers.

The chapter on Kitchen stuff might help. Also look in the Metal chapter.

Ivory

IVORY CAN BE TOO CLEAN

❖ Never wash old ivory carvings. The yellow color is pre-ferred and white ivory has a much lower value. If you have a friend whose hands perspire profusely, have that person handle the ivory, as it will add to the patina and coloring.

❖ Dust ivory with a soft cloth or brush. Buff with a clean woolen cloth.

❖ To keep ivory a warm white color, expose it to light. Ivory will darken if kept in the dark. Keep a piano open so the keys will be in natural light. Keep figurines, chess sets, and other ivory in the open.

❖ Ivory should be kept in high humidity, so it is always best to keep an open cup of water or a plant nearby.

❖ Changes in temperature may cause old ivory to crack.

❖ Don't soak ivory in water. It will soften any glue and may damage the patina.

❖ Clean ivory beads and jewelry with denatured alcohol, not water.

❖ To test ivory to see if it is real, heat the tip of a needle or pin until it is red hot. Put the point on the ivory in an inconspicuous spot. If it goes in more than a tiny pinprick, it is not ivory.

More information in the Jewelry chapter.

Jewelry

KEEP YOUR JEWELRY SPARKLING CLEAN

☞ *VALUE HINT*

A signature on a piece of jewelry adds 30 percent to the value. Look at the pin shank, pin back, and watch for the signature.

CLEANING

❖ To clean silver, gold, or diamond jewelry, soak it in a glass of vodka overnight. But remember, discard the vodka after using it; don't drink it.

❖ Clean your hard stone jewelry, the diamonds and rubies, in a mixture of equal parts liquid laundry detergent and water. Quickly swish dirty pearls, opals, or coral in a mixture of 1 teaspoon Ivory liquid and 1 quart lukewarm water. Don't soak. Rinse, pat dry.

☞ *VALUE HINT*

Gemstones are colder to the touch than glass. Colored gems like emeralds, rubies, and sapphires should not appear scratched. If there are scratches, the "stone" is probably colored glass.

❖ Do not wash rhinestones with water. It will tarnish the

foil background. Do not hold the jewelry under running water. Use a Q-Tip or small, soft brush and glass cleaner to dab away dirt. Rub dry with a soft cloth.

❖ Jet beads can be washed in mild soapsuds and water. Don't soak the strings. If the jet is carved, make a wad of soft white bread, center of the slice. The bread will absorb the dirt and grease, then crumble and fall away.

❖ Never scrub threaded coral beads. The edges of the coral are so sharp they may cut the bead string.

❖ Never wash a miniature portrait pin or hair jewelry.

JADE IS COOL

❖ You can tell a piece of jade by the feel. It will be cold, even in warm weather.

❖ For a quick shine on a silver belt buckle or large pin, try rubbing it on a piece of dark-colored carpet.

❖ To test a piece of jade to see if it is real, use a small penknife. Rub the tip of the knife across the bottom of the piece until there is a mark. A white line means the knife scratched the stone and it is not jade. A black line means the stone scratched the blade and it is probably jade.

❖ To remove verdegris (the green mold that forms on metal) from costume jewelry, mix equal amounts of mayonnaise and ketchup. Rub it on and quickly remove it. Wash. Try again and leave it longer if the first treatment didn't work. Don't use on pieces with real or fake pearls.

❖ Diamonds clean well in club soda.

☛ *VALUE HINT*

Your diamond or precious-stone jewelry, antique or modern, should be reappraised every other year.

❖ Bakelite jewelry can be cleaned with a soft damp cloth and a mild abrasive cleaner such as a car body polish. After cleaning, rub on beeswax furniture polish.

STORAGE

❖ Care of pearls is important. Don't put them in a box with sharp objects. Don't let them touch perfume or hair spray. Perspiration is bad for them, so wipe the pearls after each wearing. Don't soak a string of pearls in water; the water may weaken the string. Never store them in airtight warm places like safe-deposit boxes or plastic bags. Long periods of airtight storage will ruin the pearls' luster. It is said that pearls retain their luster best when worn by a beautiful woman.

Strings of pearls have gone up in value dramatically. If you own pearls that are more than 10 years old, have them reappraised.

❖ Ivory and opals, like pearls, need to "breathe." Do not wrap them in plastic; keep them in a cloth bag.

❖ Don't store sterling silver jewelry in cotton-filled boxes. The cotton makes it tarnish faster.

❖ Keep cuff links or earrings in foam egg cartons in your drawer.

❖ If a thin chain becomes tangled, dust it with talcum powder and the untangling will be easier.

❖ Don't wrap jewelry in a disposable tissue. You may accidentally throw it away. My aunt had a cold and accidentally threw a tissue-wrapped diamond ring out the car window. She learned the hard way: never litter!

❖ Never store rhinestone jewelry in plastic bags. Moisture inside the bag will cause the stones to discolor.

❖ Perfume and hair spray will damage amber beads, pearls, and opals.

☞ *VALUE HINT*

The women pictured on old cameos often have long thin noses. The cute turned-up nose is seen on modern cameos made after the 1920s.

REPAIR

❖ Restring old beads on dental floss. It's very strong.

❖ To repair or restring a broken seed pearl necklace, use monofilament nylon fishing line. It is strong, fine, and stiff enough to use without a needle. The original Victorian pieces were strung on horsehair.

☛ *VALUE HINTS*

Beads that are still strung on the original thread have more value than restrung pieces. If you plan to wear the jewelry, however, be sure the string has not weakened.

Rub amber beads on a wool carpet, then hold the beads over a small scrap of paper. The amber will collect static electricity and pick up the paper. Glass will not. Sometimes when amber is rubbed, it smells a bit like pine resin. Amber beads sell for higher prices than glass beads.

❖ Always remove rings before washing dishes or your hair. The rings may slide off in the soapy water and get lost down the drain.

❖ Turquoise is porous and stains easily. Remove rings and bracelets before doing dishes, cleaning, or using hand lotion or face cream.

❖ Don't wear jewelry when swimming. Both salt and chlorine damage glass and some types of natural stones. Sand will scratch coral, pearl, opal, lapis, turquoise, and other stones. Base metals will corrode. Glittering metals sometimes attract barracudas. They don't see well and they think it's the shiny underside of a sick fish.

❖ If one link in your antique gold chain breaks, be very careful. There are probably other worn links that will soon break. Look especially close at the link that holds the clasp.

The single link holding a pendant on a chain also wears thin faster than others.

❖ Check the claw settings on any antique jewelry to be sure the prongs are not worn or loose. It is cheaper to be careful than to replace lost stones. If you can "wiggle" the stone, take it to be fixed. Claw settings for precious stones can be "retipped."

❖ If you are having antique jewelry repaired, be sure the jeweler uses old stones. New ones are cut differently and will seem brighter. Pearls and turquoise change color with age.

❖ When putting on earrings in front of the bathroom mirror, be sure the sink stopper is closed. Don't risk dropping the jewelry down the drain.

☞ *VALUE HINT*

Broken silver jewelry may have melt-down value. Check to see if the metal is really silver.

❖ One antique earring can still be used. Have the jeweler make it into a stickpin, a tie tac, a charm for a bracelet, or a ring. If it is a clip-on, use it like a lapel pin; if it is for a pierced ear, attach it through the knit of a sweater. Some earrings can be hung in the center of a strand of pearls, an old-fashioned adaptation of the new "pearl enhancers." "Orphan" earrings sell well now to those who wear several earrings in each ear.

Look in the Silver chapter for more help cleaning sterling silver jewelry.

Kitchen

USE YOUR ANTIQUES TO COOK, BUT CLEAN THEM FIRST

❖ To clean an old coffee grinder, grind white rice through the mill. When the rice appears to be clean, the grinder is clean enough to use.

❖ Clean a very dirty cast-iron pot the old-fashioned way. Put it in a hot wood fire in a fireplace or barbecue pit for several hours. After it is cool, wash with hot water, soap, and a stiff scrubbing brush. Then season with oil.

❖ To cure an iron pan, rub it with solid vegetable shortening and put it in the oven at 225 degrees for 30 minutes. Remove the pan from the oven, wipe off excess shortening, and put it back in the oven. Leave it in for 30 minutes more, then turn the oven off and leave the pan in the oven until it is cool.

❖ Never put a cast-iron cooking pan in the dishwasher. Do not soak it for long. Excess water will remove the "seasoning" and food will stick to the pan. You will have to season it again.

❖ An iron frying pan should be washed with steel wool and *soap*. Food will stick and the pan will rust if you use detergent, not soap.

❖ Wipe an iron pan with mineral oil to prevent rust. Let the oil soak in for several days and then wipe it off.

❖ Clean aluminum with fine steel wool or steel wool soap pads. To remove discoloration, boil 2 teaspoons cream of tartar and 1 quart water in the pot. The acid from cooking tomatoes or rhubarb in the pot may also remove the stain.

❖ Never cook tomatoes or other acid food in a copper pot without a tin lining. Acid and copper create a poison. Don't try to make tomato aspic in an unlined copper mold.

❖ Oil your butcher-block table to keep it from splitting at the seams. Use cooking oil or walnut oil if you plan to cut food on the block, mineral oil if it will be used only as a table. You must oil it at least once a month.

❖ To remove the odor from a wooden bowl, try washing it with baking soda or vinegar, then airing it in sunlight. As a last resort, fill it with diluted household bleach. Soak the bowl for about 15 minutes, then rinse with full-strength vinegar, then clear water. If this does not remove the odor, repeat the process with a stronger solution of bleach.

☞ *VALUE HINT*

> Tin cookie cutters can be dated by the construction method. Old ones are soldered in spots, not a long thin solder joint. If the solder joins the cutting-edge piece to the back by a thin, barely visible line, it is less than 50 years old. Collectors pay a premium for old cutters. The back should be an odd shape. Early cutters were made from pieces of scrap.

❖ Don't load your dishwasher with dishes or bowls with crazed glaze, lacquered metal, bone or ivory or wood handles, or wooden wares. They should never be cleaned in a dishwasher. The hot water and strong detergent will damage them.

Other information in Glass, Graniteware, Iron, Miscellaneous, and Pottery chapters—and probably in other chapters, too.

Lacquer

LACQUERED WOOD NEEDS SPECIAL CARE

❖ Lacquered wood can be damaged by a sudden change in humidity. Keep lacquer away from heat sources, preferably in a room with high humidity.

❖ Small lacquered pieces should be displayed in a cabinet near a small open dish of water to keep the humidity level at 55 percent.

❖ A mixture of flour and olive oil can sometimes remove a dull film from a lacquered piece. Rub on the paste, then wipe and polish with a soft cloth.

Lamps

LIGHT YOUR LAMPS SAFELY

❖ Never run a lamp cord under a rug. Never put a heavy object on top of an electric cord. It is a fire hazard.

❖ Rewire any lamps in your home that are more than 15 years old. Cords crack and are a fire hazard. Never trust a "silk" cord. Replace it. They went out of style many years ago.

❖ Chandeliers can be cleaned in place with a spray cleaner made for that purpose. Cover the floor with paper or cloth to catch the drips. Then spray the chandelier. It will clean and drip dry.

❖ Parchment lampshades can be cleaned with a cloth soaked in milk. Wipe it dry with a clean cloth.

❖ To clean dirt and corrosion from old metal lamps and lanterns, use brass polish and steel wool. Or, to avoid rubbing off the nickel plating, first clean the surface with a strong household cleaner like Fantastik or 409. Then apply Naval Jelly (found in hardware stores) with a brush. Rub for several minutes with the brush. Let stand for 30 minutes and wash off. Let dry, then polish gently with steel wool.

☞ *VALUE HINT*

To be sure you have a genuine Tiffany lamp, you must find the words "Tiffany and Co." on the metal base. The glass shades were also marked "L.C. Tiffany," or just with the letters "L.C.T." According to the records of the Tiffany Company, all lamps were marked.

Leather

LEATHER, LIKE YOUR FACE, NEEDS PROPER SOAPS AND LOTIONS

❖ Don't laugh at this one. Some of the moisturizing creams that are sold at the cosmetics counter are equally useful to keep leather soft. Best are moisturizers that have shea butter as an ingredient. Dried leather purses can be rejuvenated with a treatment from a moisturizer with an oil in it. Try a small spot first—it may darken the leather.

❖ Use commercial leather cleaner to restore an old leather purse. Then rub in leather conditioner. Both products can be found at the shoe repair store.

❖ Clean a leather sofa or chair by dusting regularly. When necessary, wipe with a damp cloth dipped in detergent-free soapy water. If someone spills food on the leather, wipe it off immediately, but wipe the entire sofa to avoid a spot.

❖ Clean leather chairs, sofas, and tabletops regularly to avoid polish buildup. Wipe with a mixture of $\frac{1}{4}$ cup vinegar and $\frac{1}{2}$ cup water. Then wash the leather with saddle soap and rub briskly with a soft cloth.

❖ When polishing leather tabletops with saddle soap, apply the soap, wait 30 minutes, then buff with a cloth for a high shine.

❖ Pen marks can be removed from leather with a clear gum eraser, not a pink one.

❖ To preserve leather-bound books, first dust. Then apply a light application of leather protector (potassium lactate) with a soft cloth. After it dries, apply a little leather dressing (a mixture of lanolin and neat's-foot oil). This will deacidify the leather and keep it from becoming brittle. In a big city, repeat this every other year.

❖ Leather that crumbles to red powder has "red rot." It is caused by absorption of sulfur dioxide and cannot be stopped.

❖ Old leather saddles and other leather antiques can be safely cleaned and reconditioned at home. Wash the leather in warm water and glycerin soap. Rub with an old, soft cloth diaper. Keep replacing the dirty water. Don't be surprised at how much clean water is needed. A saddle takes about 10 gallons. Reshape any bent or creased sections while the leather is damp. Dry the leather overnight, away from sunlight. Next rub olive oil or almond oil into the leather. Dry for six hours, then apply more oil. A final polish can be added with carnauba wax applied with your fingertips. Buff with a soft cloth.

❖ Leather needs care. Keep it in a room with high humidity. Leave tabs and other stress points unsnapped to lessen tearing. Don't hang leather saddles, holsters, etc., over sharp nails; use large-diameter poles. Don't display near a heat source or in direct sunlight.

Marble
and
Alabaster

MARBLE IS TOPS

❖ Marble is porous and will absorb water vapors into the stone up to 6 inches deep. Airborne pollutants will also be absorbed, and eventually, when the marble dries, the dirt will erode or stain the surface of the marble. Avoid excess humidity. We have a white marble bust of a girl that keeps getting brown stains in the nose and ears. It was incorrectly stored in a dirty, wet garage. Cleaning it helps for only a few months.

❖ It is best to wash marble with *distilled* water. Any trace of acid or iron in tap water will cause deterioration or stains. Use soft soap, a bit of ammonia, and a plastic container.

❖ Never clean marble with either vinegar or lemon juice. They will damage the marble. If someone spills lemonade on your marble-topped table, wipe it up immediately and wash the area with ammonia and water to neutralize the acid.

❖ Stains on marble are difficult to remove. Each stain requires a different treatment. Your library has a book filled with suggestions for removing marble stains. Most stains cannot be completely removed.

❖ The marble top of a table can be shined with putty powder (zinconium oxide) from a cemetery monument works. Put the powder on a piece of damp felt and rub the marble until it shines.

❖ A good way to remove rings and stains from a white marble top is to mix TSP (trisodiumphosphate, found in paint stores), water, and scouring powder. Rub on the spots. Too much rubbing may remove some of the shine, so be careful.

❖ Never carry a marble tabletop flat. It can break under its own weight. Always carry a slab of marble with the thin edge up.

❖ Use coasters under glasses and flower vases on marble-topped tables. Marble can stain easily.

❖ Small cracks in marble can be concealed with a mixture of colored wax and chalk dust. The same mixture can be used to make a new nose or finger for a damaged marble figure.

❖ Alabaster is different. To clean alabaster, first dust with a soft brush. Then wipe with turpentine or dry-cleaning fluid. Do *not* use water. Alabaster dissolves in water. Some people like to polish alabaster with paste furniture wax, but the wax will eventually yellow slightly.

Medical

SOME ANTIQUES ARE BAD MEDICINE

❖ Be very careful when handling old bottles or medical equipment. The remains of old drugs, even toxic materials, may still cling to the surface. A broken bit of glass or a sliver could let these toxic materials reach your bloodstream.

❖ If you have unopened bottles of drugs or other pharmaceuticals, be sure to check for ether or picric acid. These can explode spontaneously and are dangerous to keep.

❖ Some very old medical mixtures include poisons, opium, and now-illegal drugs. It is best to empty and wash the bottles. Wear protective gloves.

❖ "Irradiated water" was considered a good health drink early in the century. Water was kept in radioactive pottery jugs. These jugs should not be kept in the house with people or pets. They are still radioactive. Most of these jugs were made with the name in the glaze and some sort of medical claim for the special water, so you can easily identify them.

Less threatening help for medical materials will be found in Bottles, Metal, Miscellaneous, Paper, Pottery and Porcelain, and other chapters.

Metal

NINETEENTH-CENTURY METAL WAS MADE TO SHINE

❖ Always use a metal polish on the metal it was made for. Don't clean silver with pewter or chrome polish. The wrong formulation may scratch the metal.

❖ An old cotton sock is a good polishing cloth. So is an old cloth diaper.

❖ Metal polish paste or cream cleans better than a polish-impregnated cloth if you have a very tarnished piece. Cloths are good for small metal parts with little tarnish.

❖ Metal saltshaker tops can be kept from rusting or oxidizing if they are cleaned and sprayed with a silicone product. Wax will also help.

METAL CARE

❖ Don't try to remove dents in silver or pewter. This is a job for an expert.

❖ When starting a dirty job like cleaning metal or refinishing pewter, try this trick: Rub your nails into a bar of soap. At cleanup time the dirt will easily come out from under the nail tips.

❖ If the metal top on your saltshaker won't unscrew, turn the saltshaker upside down in a small bowl of white vinegar. Let it soak for about 12 hours. The cap should then be loose. Rub soap on the inside of the cap to keep it from sticking again.

❖ Don't use a mechanical buffer to clean old silver or pewter. The heat will cause a change in the surface metals and alter the color.

❖ Chrome should be cleaned with a mild chrome cleaner, not an abrasive.

❖ Don't clean coins. Collectors want coins with the patina unchanged. Cleaning destroys the value.

❖ Lead garden sculpture should not be cleaned. The dirt and discoloration adds to the beauty of the piece. Lead is so soft that most types of cleaning will harm the finish.

Also look for cleaning tips in chapters about Advertising, Aluminum, Brass, Bronze, Chrome, Copper, Iron, Silver, etc.

Miscellaneous

A MIXED BAG

❖ Treat your antiques like your grandparents: Have proper respect for their age, but don't exaggerate their fragility.

DON'T GET STUCK

❖ When buying antiques, beware of stickers, Magic Marker numbers, or other dealer-added labels that may damage the antique. Any type of sticky tape or label will leave marks on paper or paint finishes. Metal with an oxidized finish is damaged when ink marks are removed. Pencil or pen notations often leave indentations.

❖ Mayonnaise can be used to remove old masking tape, stickers, or labels from glass or china.

Or,

❖ Try rubbing peanut butter on the sticky area until the glue is gone. Do not use this method on porous materials where the oil from the peanut butter could leave a stain.

Or,

❖ Heat a gummed label with a hair dryer. The glue will melt a bit and it will be easier to peel off the sticker.

Or, try this:

❖ Use Bestine solvent, found at art supply stores.

❖ Rubber cement solvent, available at art supply and office supply stores, has many uses. Put a few drops on a paper towel and rub ink smudges, adhesive tape glue, or label glue off glass or porcelain.

❖ Don't sticky-tape a top on a teapot. The decoration may come off with the tape. Secure a top with special dental wax.

❖ We once pulled some of the silver plating from a Sheffield candlestick when we removed the cellophane tape that held a Christmas decoration to the candlestick. A friend pulled some of the glaze from a plate when she pulled masking tape off the plate. Don't use anything with a strong glue on an antique surface.

CLEAN IT UP

❖ There are many ecologically sound products made for care and repair of antiques. Look at the labels. Our ancestors cleaned pewter with wood ashes and oil.

PLASTER WILL MELT

❖ John Rogers groups or other plaster figures should not be cleaned with water or chemicals. Remove the dirt with an art gum eraser. If the finish is destroyed, repaint the figure with a watercolor paint in a shade matching the original. Most figures were beige or gray. Visit a real John Rogers group in a museum to see the correct color.

❖ Soapstone (steatite) is a very soft mineral. To clean carvings, wash with soapy water and a soft brush. To improve the sheen, rub with jeweler's rouge. Don't use a harsh abrasive.

❖ Smoke stains can be removed from a stone fireplace with an art gum eraser. Soot on the carpet in front of the fireplace can be removed with salt. Sprinkle dry salt on the soot, wait 30 minutes, then vacuum.

❖ Dust the backs of your framed pictures once a year.

❖ Dust frequently if you live near the seashore. Salt air causes problems.

❖ Cheesecloth is a good polishing cloth.

❖ Clean Indian arrowheads with soap and water and a toothbrush only if they are very dirty. Handle arrowheads carefully—they are made of surprisingly fragile material and will break if dropped.

❖ To clean old golf clubs, use Liquid Wrench (an oil found in the hardware store) and 0000-grade steel wool. The oil should not discolor the shaft.

❖ Some repairs lower value and make the sale of an antique very difficult, if not impossible. Don't buff pewter. Don't wash ivory. Don't repaint old toys. Don't tape old paper. Don't wash oil paintings.

❖ Look in your hardware store for the new glues that can fix almost anything. Buy the proper one to fix transparent glass, porous pottery, or nonporous metals. There will be one that will work.

❖ To dust small, fragile items like flower-decorated figurines, try blowing the dust away with a handheld hair
dryer set on low. For large, sturdy items, cover the end of
the vacuum cleaner nozzle with an old nylon stocking, then
vacuum.

❖ Bugs, unfortunately, also like collections! Flies stain
paper; cockroaches eat paper and books; silverfish and firebrats damage paper, leather, and fabrics. Use proper sprays,
check often for damage, and hire professional exterminators if you have a serious problem.

❖ If you hear crickets in the house, spray with insect killer.
Crickets eat wool as well as old rugs, silks, and paper.

❖ Keep mousetraps, rat poison, and bug poison in the attic
if you store antique furniture or textiles there.

❖ Aerosol paint strippers are fast but need special precautions. Wear goggles, gloves, and a long-sleeved shirt

because the spray will float. With aerosol strippers there is no brushing and these work well on small irregular surfaces such as carvings, but large jobs are better with conventional brushed-on stripper.

❖ Fill an old pair of pantyhose with cedar shavings from the pet store. Hang it in your closet to discourage moths.

❖ Collectors in a warm, humid climate like Hawaii or Florida have special problems. If you collect metal, leather, wool, or textiles, beware! Store pieces in an airtight container or in a place with good air circulation, like a half-filled closet. Keep textiles clean and dry. Best method: after washing, dry in the sun. Use mothballs or cedar closets for textiles. Don't store items in wooden boxes that are kept on the ground; insects may burrow from below. Metal will rust if not kept away from salt air and humidity. Storage in a plastic bag is usually acceptable.

❖ Smoking is bad for the health of your antiques. Smoke causes discoloration and weakens textiles. Nicotine stains fabrics, pictures, and wood. Another reason to stop smoking!

❖ When restoring antiques, take color pictures before and after for records of colors used, exact placement of decorative details, and marks. You may need the information for insurance claims.

TREAT IT LIKE PAPER

❖ If your papier-mâché doll heads or furniture is cracking, you might try arresting the cracks with a thin coat of white household glue.

❖ Never wash papier-mâché.

☛ *VALUE HINT*

Look through the wrong end of a telescope if you plan to buy it. If it can be focused, all of the parts are there.

PLAYING POLITICS

❖ Do not regild, resilver, or repaint political buttons or badges. It lowers the value.

☛ *VALUE HINT*

Condition, size, and small details determine the value of political buttons. To be sure the description is accurate for buying, selling, or insurance, just put the buttons on the glass top of a copying machine. Make copies of both the front and the back.

DISPLAY IT RIGHT

❖ To display your compacts and other small collectibles, make metal drapery-hook stands. Bend the hooks to look like little easels.

❖ Check glass shelves regularly to be sure they have not loosened or bent.

❖ Folding fans should be stored closed. It protects the fabric.

❖ You and your antiques may have different ideas about ideal temperature and humidity. Bronzes and photographs like 40 percent humidity; stone carvings and oil paintings like 50 percent; wooden pieces and paper prefer 55 percent. The level, whatever you choose, should be constant. It can be measured by a hygrometer, which you will be able to find at a hardware store.

❖ You can check to see if the light intensity is too strong for your antique pictures and fabrics. Take a light meter used with a camera and check the exposure values (EV) and lux. The maximum level for watercolors, paper, and other easily damaged items is 50 lux. Glass, stone, and metal is safe up to 300 lux.

❖ Sunlight and heat can harm most antiques. Wood, paper, textiles, glass, ivory, leather, and many other organic materials will discolor, fade, or crack. Cover sunny windows with blinds or curtains or apply a sun-filtering plastic coating to the windows. These coatings can be found at hardware and window stores, or installed by special companies listed in the Yellow Pages. Information is available from museums or art conservators.

❖ Keep art, paintings, prints, and textiles away from sunny windows.

❖ It is said creativity comes from a messy, cluttered environment. It inspires ideas. Remember that the next time you rearrange your collectibles. Looking back at our son's room, we realize there may be a reason why he is in a creative business.

❖ Fishing line is strong and almost invisible and can be used to tie fragile items to a base or wall. This will prevent damage from earthquakes, two year olds, and dogs with wagging tails.

❖ Microcrystalline waxes, like Stick-em or the wax used by dentists to keep braces from hurting, are good to stick ceramics and glass on shelves, but don't use them on soft, unglazed ceramics like Indian pots. They may leave an oil stain.

❖ Display groups of at least three of your collectibles to get decorating impact.

❖ Never use an antique stove before it has been restored and inspected by a qualified stove dealer or repair service. A damaged stove may explode or burn and cause serious injury. Or it may give off deadly carbon monoxide fumes.

❖ Don't store old paint rags. They may ignite spontaneously.

❖ If you discover a cache of very dirty antiques and you are not dressed in work clothes, make yourself a temporary cover-up from a plastic garbage bag.

❖ Be sure to dispose of paint thinners, harsh chemical cleaners, and other dangerous products in the ecologically approved manner. Don't just dump them in the sewer.

❖ Wear rubber gloves when handling bleaching materials, poisonous materials, strong solvents, or harsh chemicals.

❖ Never move an object that might explode. Call the local police bomb squad. Many accidents are caused by old souvenir hand grenades and firearms. Don't keep old bullets in a hot attic.

❖ Always keep firearms locked up, even antique ones. Old guns should have the barrels filled so it is impossible to accidentally discharge them.

❖ Watch out for exploding antiques! Any type of gun, shell, powder can, and nitrate movie film, and some chemicals possibly left in old bottles or cans, are dangerous. If you don't know about these items, contact your local police or fire department for help.

❖ If you have an instant-on television set, beware! The instant-on works because a current is always running through the set, even when it is off. This means more power is used, the set wears out faster, and, most serious for the collector, there is a greater risk of fire. Next time the set needs repair, ask the serviceman to remove the instant-on feature. If you use a remote unit to turn off the set, the same dangers exist.

❖ Check the metal strips holding any heavy wall-hung shelves once a year. After a few years, a heavy load will cause "creep" and the metal brackets will bend. When the posts bend, the shelving will fall and down will come vases, dishes, and all.

❖ If you live in an earthquake area, a few precautions may help limit damage. Be sure there is a lip on the edge of a shelf that holds dishes and glassware. Use dental wax (an orthodontist uses it with braces) to stick the objects to the shelf. String a fishing line across the front of a shelf holding baskets or other very light objects to help keep them from falling. Keep cabinet doors locked shut so pieces will not fall out. Magnetic "childproof" locks help some also.

GET-A-BARGAIN SHOPPING

❖ The best time to buy an antique is when you see it.

❖ If it seems too good to be true, it usually is! Trust your instincts when buying antiques. Experienced collectors notice many little signs of repair or reproduction, often without realizing it.

❖ When the weather is bad, the auction or flea market will probably be good. Brave storms and cold and attend events in bad weather when the crowd is small and the prices

low. Dealers at one stormy outdoor show kept offering us "rain prices."

❖ Go to antique shows early; there may be plenty of antiques left at the end of the show but the dealers are tired and not as eager to talk to the customers. Or go late. They may sell at a bargain to avoid packing the piece for a trip.

❖ Never bid at an auction if you have not previewed the items.

☛ *VALUE HINT*

"Never invest your money in anything that eats or needs repainting." Wise words from Billy Rose, a successful showman and art collector.

MOVING?

❖ Moving is a collector's nightmare. Rolls of paper that schools use to cover lunch tables is the best wrap. Cut the paper to different sizes before starting to pack. Put paper plates between plates. Wrap saucers 10 to 15 together at one time. Put paper napkins between the cover of a teapot and the upside-down lid. Toilet paper tubes are good holders for mustard spoons or ladles. Disposable diapers are best for large items. Get commercial picture boxes from the moving company to transport paintings.

❖ If you are having your antiques moved in a van to a new home, watch out for damage. Check the antiques as they are unloaded. Sweep the inside of the moving van and save any small pieces of veneer or wood that might have chipped off your furniture.

❖ Be sure copies of lists of valuables, photographs, and other information can be found in case of an insurance loss. Give copies to a trusted friend or keep them in your safe-deposit box.

❖ Moving your own belongings? Be careful about insurance. Rental trucks or your car may have coverage for antiques that is too low. Your homeowner's policy probably does not cover damage from poor packing. Check with your agent before you move!

❖ When moving, remember there is usually no insurance coverage for breakage if the items are not packed by the shipper.

❖ Pack plates to be moved on their side, with a pad under and between the plates. The weight of a stack of plates can crack the bottom plates.

❖ Don't stack cups. If you must do it, separate every two cups with a piece of paper or felt.

❖ Before you have a garage or tag sale, check with your insurance agent. If necessary, get short-term liability coverage. Be sure your theft coverage is adequate.

❖ If you have to pack or store an oddly shaped antique, a footed bowl, or an unsteady figurine, try this trick: Dampen a polyurethane sponge, preferably the two-layer type with a stiffer bottom layer. Put the antique piece on the wet sponge. It will make the proper-shaped indentation and when the sponge dries, the piece will be held safely in one position.

THE RIGHT NOTE FOR MUSICAL CARE

❖ Beware of moths in your piano. They sometimes set up housekeeping, eat, and lay eggs in the interior fabrics. Use normal household moth killers.

❖ Piano keys can be cleaned with yogurt. *(More help is in the chapter about Ivory.)*

❖ Never stop a music box in the middle of a tune. If the box is later moved, there is more likely to be damage to the spikes on the cylinder if it is not at the end of a song.

❖ Be very careful if you try to oil the mechanism of a music box. Too much oil will cause damage.

❖ Never try to play a disc on your music box that was not made for that box. The machine will be damaged and the disc ruined.

RECORDS

❖ The playing surface of old phonograph records should never be touched by a bare hand. The records should be stored and packed vertically to prevent warping. Keep away from extremes of heat or cold.

❖ You might be able to remove the warp from a 78 rpm record. Put it between two pieces of glass in a sunny window for a day. Let it cool. This should straighten the record.

☛ *VALUE HINT*

Don't get too excited if your violin has the label of Antonius Stradivarius. It has been forged and appears in many 19th- and 20th-century violins of low value. One type of labeled violin was originally offered in the Sears catalog for $7.

Paintings and Pictures

FINE ART NEEDS FINE CARE

❖ Don't hang an oil painting above a fireplace that is used. Smoke will damage the painting.

❖ If possible, hang oil paintings on an inside wall away from direct sunlight.

❖ Leave a small air space between the wall and the back of a painting to allow air to flow. "Bumpers" to put on the back of pictures are available at frame shops.

❖ Paintings displayed in a dining room often are spattered with food and sometimes pick up the odors of the food. They will eventually need to be cleaned.

❖ Don't try to clean an oil painting unless you are an expert. You can do permanent damage. Go to a restorer who cleans oil paintings.

❖ Never, never wash an oil painting; it will dull the colors and may damage the canvas. Never rub an oil polish on an oil painting; it will darken with age. Never try to remove dust with a vacuum cleaner; it may also remove bits of paint.

❖ A miniature painting should not be washed. Most miniatures are painted on ivory and the paint will wash off.

❖ Never wash, or even wipe or dust, a watercolor or pastel. Don't even shake the picture.

❖ Have your paintings "rekeyed" if the canvas seems to be loose. There are small wooden wedges or "keys" at the back of the frame that stretch the canvas. Have a professional framer do the job.

❖ Flies are not toilet-trained and they leave bits of their meals on pictures and paintings. These flyspecks can be carefully removed with a knife blade.

❖ If you must move a painting in a car trunk, be careful. Put cardboard on each side of the canvas to keep it from being punctured by a tool or holder in the trunk. Close the trunk lid slowly. A quick slam may build up the air pressure and rip the canvas. If going on a long trip through several temperature zones, remember that a very hot, then very cold trunk temperature will damage the painting.

❖ If there is no wall space or vertical space left for extra paintings, store them under the bed, face down. It's dark, has good air circulation, and the paintings can be kept horizontal without fear of damage from feet.

❖ The best place to store paintings is in a closet with no exterior walls. The temperature and humidity levels will be the best in your house.

❖ Try not to store an old painting-on-canvas flat and face up on a floor. The paint may crack at the stretcher. A dog may step on it. Store it upright.

Or,

❖ Decorators now show rooms filled with rows of pictures stacked against the wall, or on special shelves or mantels. Doesn't seem to be a problem that only parts of each picture can be seen!

FRAME IT, HANG IT, CLEAN IT

❖ Never spray liquid glass cleaner directly on the glass in a picture frame. The dripping liquid may fall behind the glass and stain the picture. Spray the cleaning cloth, then rub the glass with the damp cloth.

❖ Use eyeglass-cleaning tissues to clean the glass on small pictures.

❖ Never touch the surface of a watercolor or drawing. Lift unframed paper by the corners.

❖ When framing a charcoal or pastel drawing, avoid plastic; use real glass. The plastic will pick up static electricity and actually pull the charcoal or pastel dust off the paper.

❖ Check the safety of wires and screw eyes before hanging an old picture.

❖ Worried about where to hang a picture? Put a small dot of toothpaste on the top corners of the frame and press the frame against the wall so the toothpaste leaves a mark. If the position looks O.K., then pound in the hook and wipe off the toothpaste. Don't do this if the wall is papered.

❖ Look behind all hanging pictures once a year to be sure there are no insect nests, dust, or loose wires.

Paper

DO PAPER RIGHT

❖ Although paper is acid and deteriorates, ink fades, and insects and light cause damage, it is still possible to preserve paper antiques. Keep paper dry, cool, sealed away from oxygen and ultraviolet light. Mylar plastic bags are the best. Important papers should be deacidified by an expert. Dirt and other damage can be repaired.

❖ All types of light—sunlight, fluorescent light, and electric light—will eventually harm paper.

❖ Excessive humidity will cause mold on paper. Keep the humidity level between 45 and 55 percent.

☞ *VALUE HINT*

A heavy odor from smoke or mildew lowers the value of a collection of paper.

❖ Wash your hands before handling old paper collectibles. Museum personnel wear white cotton gloves. Hands can damage paper collectibles by leaving fingerprints, or traces of oil or salt. All will cause stains eventually.

❖ To clean old paper, try talcum powder. Take a soft brush or powder puff, sprinkle on the powder, leave for an hour, and brush it off.

❖ Clean dirty postcards with a piece of white bread. Be sure to cut the crust off first.

❖ Use lighter fluid on a cloth to gently rub grease pencil marks off paper.

❖ Remove old staples, rubber bands, paper clips, etc., from paper objects. They can stain the paper.

❖ Never fold old paper.

❖ To remove wrinkles from old paper, set a regular iron for cotton. Iron out the wrinkles from the wrong side of the paper. Be sure to iron quickly so you do not scorch the paper.

☛ *VALUE HINT*

Date business cards and other advertising from telephone numbers and Zip Codes. Phone numbers were first used in 1878. Fewer than seven digits dates the card from 1878 to the 1940s. Letters and numbers were used until the 1950s. Area codes were introduced in 1951. Zip Codes were in use by 1963. Postal zones, one- or two-digit numbers, were used from 1943 to 1963. The nine-digit Zip started in 1980.

❖ Do not use cellophane tape or other sticky tapes on paper. Even if the tape is removed, the paper will eventually discolor from the contact with the glue.

❖ Do not use Post-its or similar sticky paper notes on books, papers, or catalogs. Eventually the bits of remaining glue will discolor, especially on glossy-finish paper.

❖ Paper must "breathe." Don't glue it to a backing. It expands and contracts and eventually it will tear.

❖ Do not mount old maps, prints, etc., on cardboard. The acid in the cardboard will cause stains. Use an all-rag board. An art store can help.

❖ When framing paper documents and prints: no glue, tape, or rubber cement. No scissors—don't trim anything. No pencils or pens, and don't try to rewrite an autograph. No staples or clips. No extremes of temperature or humidity. No direct sunlight—it fades the ink.

❖ Keep prints in the best shape by dusting picture frames and glass with a feather duster. This discourages airborne mold spores that might work their way under the glass.

❖ To take desirable cards from an old scrapbook or to remove old wallpaper from a box, soak the entire piece in warm water until the paste loosens. Most types of early ink will survive this method, but test ink on handwritten pages before soaking. Also test dark wallpapers. They may bleed.

MATCHLESS COLLECTORS

❖ Smelly match covers can be deodorized. Wipe front and back and remove any mildew. Put a thin layer of borax powder or cat litter in a tray, cover with flat match covers, and sprinkle on more borax. The odor will leave in a few days.

Or,

❖ Put the matchboxes in a covered box with some unwrapped bars of unscented soap. Turn them over each week. Leave them for a month. This should work for any small paper items.

❖ Never cut a matchbook or paste the matchbook into a scrapbook. It destroys the value. Remove the staple and the matches.

☞ *VALUE HINT*

The value of a match cover is lowered by writing or marks, scrapes or gouge marks from a carelessly removed staple, or a damaged or missing striker.

STORING PAPER

❖ Never store old paper collectibles in ordinary cardboard boxes or plastic bags. Buy the acid-free boxes and Mylar wrapping film that are approved for long-term storage. Many picture-framing, photography, and art supply stores will have these items.

❖ Never store paper items in damp cellars or basements. Try to keep the humidity below 70 degrees, preferably around 50 degrees.

❖ If you store paper ephemera like trade cards or labels in notebooks or photo albums, be sure to open the albums several times a year to let the air circulate. Use albums with acid-free paper.

❖ Paper and glue are a feast to many bugs like cockroaches and firebrats. Spray often and check for damage. Hire a professional exterminator if you notice insect damage.

SAVE THE LABEL

❖ If there are traces of glue on the back of a label you want to save, soak the label and carefully scrape the glue off under water. Then dry flat. If you have coated or foil paper labels, do not soak them. Dampen the back only to remove glue or flatten the label.

❖ To remove tape or labels from a paperback book or pamphlet, put it on a flat surface and pour lighter fluid on the tape. Wipe off the fluid in five seconds. Drip a little more fluid on the tape. Pry loose a bit of the label or tape with a letter opener or dull knife and lift up the edge. Continue to pry loose, lift the flap, and pour fluid until the label is off. The fluid dissolves the glue. Go slowly; if the glue is not soft enough, you may tear the paper.

Don't ignore other tips in Advertising, Baseball Cards, Books, Bottles, Miscellaneous, and other chapters.

```
┌─────────────────────────────────────────┐
│  ╔═══════════════════════════════════╗   │
│  ║                                   ║   │
│  ║       Paperweights                ║   │
│  ║                                   ║   │
│  ╚═══════════════════════════════════╝   │
└─────────────────────────────────────────┘
```

Paperweights

WEIGHTY PROBLEMS

❖ Be careful about displaying paperweights or other heavy objects on glass shelves. With each new purchase you add more weight to the display shelf, until one day there is a crash and the shelf and weights are damaged. It may be safe for years, but a slight jar from a slamming door may be enough to cause the glass to crack. Also, a word of warning about wall-hung shelves on metal strips: These develop "creep" and after several years may pull loose at the top and eventually collapse.

❖ If using a glass shelf to display a paperweight collection, be sure it is strong enough. The ideal size is 18 inches long, 4 inches deep, and at least $\frac{1}{4}$ inch thick. Glass will become more brittle with age.

❖ Scratched glass paperweights can be professionally polished with little loss of value. Cracks and deep nicks cannot be repaired.

❖ Snow domes are liquid-filled paperweights. They should not be stored in the dark. Exposure to light is necessary to keep the liquid clear.

❖ Snow domes or glass paperweights that are displayed on a wooden table in front of a sunny window may magnify the sun's rays enough to scorch the tabletop.

❖ If the liquid in a snow dome gets cloudy or has partially evaporated, it is very difficult to replace it. Snow domes with black plastic bases or brown pottery bases made in the 1930s and 1940s can be opened and repaired. The dome is held in place by plaster of Paris, which can be carefully chipped away. Domes with new shiny black plastic bases, black pottery bases (1940s), or cobalt blue bases (1920s) cannot be opened unless they are some of the few screw-type examples.

❖ Rub tartar-control toothpaste on your scratched snow dome paperweights. It will remove the smaller scratches.

❖ A cracked snow dome paperweight cannot be fixed.

More help in the Glass and Plastic chapters.

Pens

CLEAN IT *WRITE*

❖ Soak dirty pen points in all-purpose liquid household cleanser. After about 12 hours the metal should be clean.

❖ Replacement ink sacs are available at stores that sell expensive pens or from pen restorers.

☛ *VALUE HINT*

Pen collectors look for quality workmanship. A gold pen nib is good. The iridium ball fused to the nib should be intact. The filling system should work or have only a minor problem like a bad ink sac. Large pens usually bring higher prices than small ones.

Pewter

POLISH THE PEWTER

❖ Clean pewter with commercial pewter polish. Never use scouring powder or steel wool.

❖ Some say they rub cabbage leaves on pewter to clean it.

❖ Don't clean badly tarnished pewter with lye unless you are aware of the physical dangers involved. The pewter won't be hurt, but you might be.

❖ Pewter looks best when displayed against a blue background.

Also read the chapter on Metal.

Photography

PICTURE-PERFECT COLLECTIBLES

❖ Don't display photographs in direct sunlight. If labeling the back of a picture, use a pencil or china marker, not a felt-tipped pen. Don't use cellophane tape, staples, or paper clips. Don't mount in a sticky photo album. Don't store in an area with rapid temperature or humidity changes.

❖ If the photograph album you plan to buy smells like plastic, don't take it. The fumes will eventually destroy the pictures.

❖ Proper storage of old photographs is important because they can be damaged by acidic paper, glue on envelope seams, ink from ballpoint pens, chemicals in glassine, moisture that can collect in plastic sleeves, etc.

❖ Never store photographs with rubber bands or paper clips. Store them in acid-free boxes and envelopes, available at stores and through mail-order catalogs.

❖ Never touch the surface of a daguerreotype or an ambrotype. The perspiration will stain the image.

❖ When storing unframed tintypes, first dust them carefully with a soft brush. Put each one in a separate acid-free envelope with the image side away from the envelope seam.

Label the envelope with pencil or India ink before inserting the tintype. Do not flex or bend the tintype because it might crack. If the tintype is mounted in an old cardboard mat or daguerreotype case, keep it in the case and then store the framed tintype in the envelope.

❖ Daguerreotype cases can be polished with liquid shoe wax (not polish).

❖ If you have an old, valuable tintype or photograph, have a copy made. Display the copy, and keep the original away from sunlight and dirt.

There may be more suggestions in the Paper chapter.

Plastic and Celluloid

SPECIAL CARE FOR PLASTIC

❖ Plastic should be cleaned gently. Wipe with a damp cloth, then dry. Do not use an abrasive cleaner. Soapy water can be used.

❖ Clean 1920s celluloid with a paste of vinegar and flour. Rub, wait a few minutes, then rinse and dry. If this doesn't work, try using a paste of dishwashing detergent and warm water. Don't press hard or the celluloid will dent.

❖ When cleaning old hairbrushes backed with celluloid, do not plunge the brushes in a sink full of water. If water collects between the brush and the plastic, it will cause damage. Never keep in direct sunlight. Celluloid, or cellulose nitrate, is flammable.

❖ Plastic furniture from the 1950s often scratches. A good polishing with automobile wax might help cover the blemishes.

❖ When storing plastic toys and novelties like PEZ containers, keep them away from heat. They might melt. Don't store plastic items touching each other. The different types sometimes react, causing damage.

❖ Molded plastic parts of toys, computers, and dishes will become brittle and deteriorate when exposed to ultraviolet light. Plastic often yellows, and although there are several products that may improve the appearance of discolored plastic, there has not been a major study to decide the best type of care. For now it is best to keep plastic away from strong lights and pollution.

Pottery
and
Porcelain

DISHING OUT INSTRUCTIONS

❖ If you have a lightweight vase that tips easily, fill it with sand.

❖ Think about the problems of owning a cat and a large collection of ceramics!

❖ Do not put water in a pottery container with an unglazed interior. The water will be absorbed and eventually stain the container.

❖ Quick cure for a leaking flower vase: Coat the outside and inside with clear silicone household glue. Coat again if it still leaks.

❖ If you want to use a valuable porcelain punch bowl at a party, try this: Buy a piece of lightweight clear plastic hose at a hardware store. Slit the hose and use it to protect the rim of the bowl from the punch ladle.

❖ Good tips for use of Fiesta ware and any other heavy, color-glazed dishes of the 1930s. Most, like Bauer, are oven-safe for baking—up to 350 degrees. Do not use in a microwave. Do not use on a direct flame. Do not wash in an automatic dishwasher; the detergent may discolor the glaze. Do not scour. Store with felt between stacked plates to avoid scratching. Early 1930 to 1942 dishes had lead in the glaze, so do not use scratched dishes with acidic foods. Lead poisoning is possible with prolonged use. Radon danger has been suggested but is unlikely in a well-ventilated house.

❖ A hair dryer set on cool can be used to blow the dust off very ornate pieces of porcelain.

☛ VALUE HINT

Figurines are often damaged. Examine the fingers, toes, and other protruding parts for damage or repairs.

❖ Don't use rubber gloves when washing figurines with protruding arms and legs. The gloves may snag and cause damage.

❖ Don't scrub gilding and gold edges on porcelains.

❖ When cleaning ceramics, be sure to remove your rings so you don't scratch the dishes. Wear tight sleeves to avoid snagging a figurine's arms or legs. Hold pieces with both hands. Don't pick up a teapot by its handle or spout.

❖ Rinse food off plates as soon after use as possible to avoid stains.

❖ China can be washed in warm water with mild soapsuds. The addition of ammonia to the water will add that extra sparkle.

❖ Always wash antique china in a sink lined with a rubber mat or towels. This helps prevent chipping. Wash one piece at a time. Rinse and let it air-dry.

❖ Modern bleach can damage 18th-century and some 19th-century dishes. To clean old dishes, try hydrogen peroxide or bicarbonate of soda. Each removes a different type of stain.

❖ Stains on porcelains can be removed by soaking in a mixture of 2 tablespoons Polident denture cleaner in 1 quart tepid water.

❖ Rub salt inside old tea and coffee cups to remove stains.

❖ Some tea and coffee stains can be removed by rubbing them with damp baking soda.

❖ To clean ironstone and other porous pottery, use wig bleach from a beauty parlor.

❖ The material used to make repairs is warmer to the touch than the porcelain. Feel the surface of a figurine to see if there are unseen repairs. Repairs may "dissolve" if washed in water. If you suspect a piece has been repaired, do not wash it. Clean with a soft brush dampened in a solution of ammonia and water.

❖ Several types of glue are needed to repair broken pottery and porcelain. Commercial glues found in a local hardware store are often satisfactory. Read the labels. Some types work only with pieces that are porous, others only with pieces that are not porous. Instant glue is difficult to use if the break is complicated.

☛ VALUE HINT

If the name "England" (or that of some other country) appears, the dish was probably made after 1891, but it may have been made as early as 1887. The words "made in England" (or some other country) indicate the piece was made after 1914.

❖ It is easy to glue pieces of broken china. Use a new fast-setting but not instant glue. Position the pieces correctly, then use tape to hold the parts together. If the piece needs special support, lean it in a suitable position in a box filled with sand.

❖ Glue broken china with an invisible mending cement that is waterproof.

❖ Repairs on standing figures or pitchers should be made from the bottom up.

❖ For emergency repairs to chipped pottery, try coloring the spot with a wax crayon or oil paint. It will look a little better.

❖ Clean the silver decorations on Argenta ware, made by Gustavsberg of Sweden, with commercial silver polish.

❖ Be careful about putting antique china in the dishwasher. Porcelains with gold overglaze decoration often lose the gold. Damaged or crazed glaze will sometimes pop off the plates in large pieces.

❖ Wash Sumida ware, a Japanese pottery, carefully. The orange-red color is only lightly fired and will wash off.

❖ A Grueby vase can be cleaned with a nylon scouring pad and a mild abrasive such as Softscrub. After it dries, rub a little Vaseline or mineral oil on the surface, then wipe it off. This system works for any matte-glazed pottery.

❖ Iridescent pottery like Sicardo should be carefully cleaned. Wash in mild detergent and water. Rinse. Dry by buffing vigorously with dry, fluffy towels. Then polish with a silver cloth as if it were made of metal. Buff again with a clean towel.

❖ Never use bleach on luster-decorated pottery. It will destroy the luster effect.

❖ Lusterware requires special handling because it can wear away if it is improperly washed. The ware should be washed in warm water with a mild soap or detergent. Do not rub too hard, or you will remove the luster glaze.

STORING

❖ Never stack cups or bowls inside each other.

❖ Cups are best stored by hanging them on cup hooks. Stacking cups inside each other can cause chipping.

❖ Don't store dishes for long periods of time in old newspaper wrappings. The ink can make indelible stains on china.

❖ Plastic bubble wrap can ruin the glaze on old ceramics. If the wrap touches the piece for a long time in a hot storage area, it may discolor the glaze or adhere to the surface in an almost permanent glob.

❖ When stacking dinner plates, put pieces of felt or paper between the plates. Never put more than 24 in one stack.

☛ *VALUE HINT*

A vase that has been drilled for a lamp, even if the hole for the wiring is original, is worth 30 to 50 percent the value of the same vase without a hole.

Purses

❖ Use Simichrome polish to carefully clean unlined metal mesh bags. *Unpainted, unlined* mesh bags can also be cleaned in a solution of equal parts ammonia and liquid laundry detergent. Swish the bag up and down in the mixture. Rinse, then dry with a hair dryer to keep rust from forming.

☞ *VALUE HINT*

To date a mesh purse, look at the bottom edge. If it is zigzagged or fringed, it dates from the 1920 –1930 period.

❖ An old leather purse will look better after it has been rubbed with leather cleaner, then leather conditioner. Your shoe repair shop will have several brands.

❖ Store leather purses and suitcases in a dry place with some fresh air. Damp, stagnant air encourages mold growth.

❖ Cracked plastic purses cannot be repaired.

And don't forget to look in the Leather chapter.

Rugs

THE FLOOR SHOW

❖ Turn or move a rug periodically to avoid worn spots in major traffic areas.

❖ Turn a rug a quarter or half turn twice a year so it will wear evenly.

❖ Turn over reversible rugs once a year. Turn rugs end-to-end in the room at least every three years. If the room is sunny, turn the rug several times a year to even out sun-fading.

❖ Take care of your old rug! Be sure it lies flat, preferably with an underpadding exactly the size of the rug. Move furniture and clean under legs to avoid moths.

❖ Always use a pad under a rug. It will keep any rug color from seeping onto the floor below.

❖ There are two kinds of pads to use under a rug. One type is used for a rug kept on the floor. The other is for a rug put over carpet. Ask at your rug store.

❖ There are several different types of nonskid mats that are made to be used under a rug to keep the rug in place on a tile or wooden floor.

❖ Don't shake dirt out of a small rug. The whipping action will break small fibers and loosen the knots.

❖ Use castor cups under the legs of chairs to protect carpets. They can be found at the hardware store.

❖ If heavy furniture legs have left dents in the carpet, put an ice cube on the spot and wait for it to spring back.

❖ One moth can lay 300 eggs. Each egg will hatch into a larva that eats 15 times its body weight in wool. If you see a single flying moth, you probably have a family. Look under rugs regularly for signs of damage, tunnels, or tufts of wool. If you find any, have all of your carpets and rugs cleaned. Remove any jute padding. Spray baseboards and moldings for insects. Have all your own woolen clothes dry-cleaned. Do all of this at the same time to be sure to find all of the larvae or eggs.

❖ Store a rug by rolling it; never fold it.

❖ Never store a rug in a plastic bag. The fibers need to breathe. Wrap the rug in a clean white sheet. Don't store rugs in a hot attic.

CLEANING

❖ Sprinkle salt or dry cornstarch on a rug or carpet, then vacuum to remove the dirt.

❖ To remove fresh food stains from rugs and upholstery, sprinkle cornmeal on the spot. It will act as a blotter. Then vacuum.

❖ If you spill something on your rug, rinse around the stain immediately with warm water or the stain may set and be impossible to remove.

❖ Tea stains on rugs can be removed with soda water, red wine stains with white wine, grease with a solvent. Gum should be hardened with an ice cube, then scraped off.

❖ Clean your rug the old-fashioned way. Put it face down in clean snow. After a short while, gently shake the snow off. You will be surprised at the dirt that is removed.

❖ When vacuuming an Oriental rug, don't push the sweeper too close to the fringe. Leave about 6 inches. The vacuum may catch a thread and pull it.

☞ *VALUE HINT*

> If the border of an Oriental rug is badly frayed or missing, it dramatically lowers the value. A rug with a good fringe could be worth $1,500; without a border, the same rug could be worth only $100.

❖ Most Oriental rugs can be professionally cleaned or washed. There are many books in the public library that give detailed instructions. Don't do it yourself if the rug is silk or if a test shows the colors will run. Don't worry if the rug becomes stiff when soaked in water. It will soften when dry.

❖ Never steam-clean an old Oriental rug. It will remove the natural lanolin in the wool. Wash the rug with mild soap and water.

❖ Never treat an old Oriental rug with a stain-resistant product. It will interfere with the natural lanolin in the wool.

☞ *VALUE HINT*

> Oriental rugs are graded for quality by dealers. In most cases the quality is determined by the knot count over a measured distance on the width of a rug. A 90 line count for a Chinese rug means if 1 foot of the width is marked off there will be 90 knots. Pakistani rugs have quality measured by counting knots on 1 inch of the width and 1 inch of the length, so it might be 16/18.

Rag rugs

❖ Don't dry-clean a rag rug. It should be carefully washed.

❖ Support a wet rag rug on an old bedsheet. The weight of the wet rags may tear the rug.

❖ Turn your rag rug upside down the day before you plan to clean it. Some of the loose dirt will fall out.

❖ Rugs or tapestries can be hung as wall decorations with strips of Velcro. Sew one strip to the rug, attach another to a strip on the wall. Be sure to use a strip that is exactly the width of the hanging.

❖ Wool rugs that are hung on the wall should be treated with moth repellent, perhaps even put in the sun for a few hours in the spring and fall.

Lots of suggestions that may help are in the Textiles chapter.

Security

**THE MOST IMPORTANT WAY TO PRESERVE YOUR COL-
LECTION IS TO KEEP IT SAFE FROM FIRE, THEFT, AND
DAMAGE**

❖ Protect your home and antiques from theft. Use a timer
on your lights at all times, even when you are at home. This
will set a pattern of certain lights going on and off each day.
When you are away, the house will appear to have normal
activity.

❖ If possible, when you are away, leave a car parked near
the front of the house. The car will block your driveway so
a burglar cannot load up through your garage.

❖ Have someone keep your trash cans filled. This will
help to make the house look occupied. Keep the grass
mowed and the snow shoveled. Stop your mail and paper
deliveries.

❖ If garage windows are painted, burglars won't be able to
tell if cars are home or not. Use translucent paint to get light
in the closed garage, if it has an entrance to your house.

❖ When you go away on a driving trip, be sure to cover the
window in your garage door, so the missing car won't be
noticed. New garage doors usually have no window at all,
for security reasons.

❖ When you cancel your paper before you leave on a trip, don't tell why you want the paper stopped. Call to restart it when you return.

❖ Lower the sound of your telephone bell so that it can't be heard outside when you are away on a long trip.

❖ Have one of the neighbors park their car in your driveway. Your house will look occupied and the car will be seen coming and going.

❖ Get a big mailbox so when you are away your mail will not be seen from the street.

❖ Wave and call good-bye to "Grandma and the kids" when leaving in a cab for the airport. Make it sound as if the house will be occupied.

LIGHTEN UP

❖ A photoelectric cell can be put into an existing exterior light to turn the light on at dusk, off at dawn. Another kind of adapter will turn a light on when there is motion in your yard.

❖ Light your yard so that some of the lights face the garage door and light up the entrances to the house. Put the lights high enough to be out of easy reach.

❖ Don't turn on the porch light if you will be gone for a long time. It tells everyone that you are away. Install a photocell light that automatically turns on at dusk, off at daylight, or install a gas light.

❖ Floodlights facing toward the house are better protection than floodlights facing away from the house. Moving figures and shadows can be seen more easily.

❖ If you have an alarm system, program a strobe light attached to the outside of the house to go on if there is a break-in attempt. The light will frighten the burglar and will make it easy for the police to find the house.

☛ *VALUE HINT*

August is the peak month for residential burglaries. April has the fewest home break-ins. Most home burglaries occur in the daytime. The average break-in lasts 17 minutes.

NAME AND NUMBERS

❖ Go outside and try to read your house numbers from the street. If you can't read them, get new, larger ones. Police or fire trucks responding to an emergency must be able to see the numbers in your address.

❖ Put the street number in reflecting numerals more than 3 inches high, in clear view.

❖ Don't put your name on your mailbox, front door mat, or screen door. It helps burglars find your phone number, then find out when you are away.

❖ You can list only your phone number and not your street address in the local phone book. Ask your phone company.

LOCK IT

❖ Lock your doors. There is a 12 percent chance that your home will be burglarized in the next five years. In the next fifteen years, the odds are 33 percent; in thirty years, 50 percent. And that assumes there is no increase in the rate of burglaries nationwide.

❖ Lock your doors and windows. In over 65 percent of all home burglaries, the burglar enters through a door. Most often the door was unlocked.

☛ *VALUE HINT*

The average burglar spends 60 seconds breaking into a house. If you can delay them with bars, locks, or other security measures, they may become impatient and leave.

❖ Install locks on all garage doors and windows.

❖ If you live in an old house and the locks are old, check the new types. There have been many improvements, and new locks provide much better security.

❖ Window sash locks are available at hardware stores for less than $10 each. Keep your windows closed and locked when you are out of the house.

❖ All outside doors should be made of solid wood or metal.

❖ Have a window or a peephole in every outside door.

❖ To avoid break-ins, be sure the hinges for your exterior doors are on the interior side of the door.

❖ Windows in outside doors should be covered with grill-work or made of unbreakable glass.

❖ If you feel you need added security and you don't want to use grillwork, there is a transparent film that can be applied to the window making it impossible to break the glass. Be sure you still have some possible exits in case of fire.

❖ If you have a large exposed window, put up glass shelves and fill them with inexpensive, colorful bottles. A burglar would have to break all of it, with accompanying noise, to get in.

❖ Remove the handles from jalousie or casement windows to make them more burglarproof.

❖ Put alarms on second-floor windows that are above bay window roofs or porches.

❖ Decorate with the neighborhood burglar in mind. Large windows can be made less attractive to intruders if you put shelves holding plants or collectibles across the window. Decorative shelves and grilles are made for this. Of course, be sure you can open the windows in case of fire.

❖ Use opaque window shades or drapes so the contents of your rooms can't be seen from outside.

❖ Rearrange your furniture so valuable silver or paintings can't be seen from the street.

❖ Think about security when you landscape your house. Cut bushes low under windows. Don't plant trees or bushes near doors where prowlers could hide. Place decorative lights in the yard to illuminate windows and doors. You might try the early 19th-century style of landscaping in the Midwest farm areas—no shrubbery plantings, but flowers near the house.

❖ The best burglary protection is a dog. Inmates from three Ohio prisons were surveyed and said timed lights, dead-bolt locks, and alarms are deterrents, but the thing most avoided by a thief is a noisy dog. You can buy a gadget that barks like a dog if someone comes near your front door.

❖ The best defense against a burglary is a nosy neighbor.

❖ Get an automatic dialer on your bedside phone and program the police number so you can push a button for help.

❖ Never run an ad that says "Call after 6 P.M." It is an announcement that you are away from the house during the day.

❖ Get an automatic dialer on your bedside phone and program the police number so you can push a button for help.

❖ Don't put a message on your answering machine that says you are away right now or that tells when you will return. It is best to have a message recorded by a male voice.

❖ In snowy weather, make tracks both in and out of your door. One set of tracks leaving the house is an invitation to an intruder. Or perhaps you could walk out of the house backward.

❖ Pet doors should be less than 6 inches across to keep out small children who might then open a regular door for a burglar. Old-fashioned milk chute doors should be sealed or made too small for a child to squirm through.

❖ If you are painting your house, do not leave ladders leaning on the building or piled up near the house. Chain and lock the ladders so the casual burglar can't use them. Trim your trees to make access to the roof more difficult.

❖ If you display your collection at a library, museum, or commercial store, do not let the display include your street address or city name. It's best not even to include your name. A display is an open invitation to a thief. Be sure the collection will be guarded and fully insured.

❖ Don't brag about the value of your collection to strangers. It might lead to extra interest by the local burglary groups.

KEY CHAIN RULES

❖ Don't keep identification on your key ring. If it is lost, it's an invitation for burglars to visit your home.

❖ Keep your keys on a pull-apart chain so the house keys and car keys can be separated when you leave the car in a parking lot. Never leave your house keys on the car ring when you give the car to a parking attendant.

❖ Don't keep a house key in an obvious spot in the garage or yard. Don't hide keys over the door, under the mat, under the steps, or in the mailbox. There are several types of key holders that will let you hide keys in better ways. Some are magnetic, some look like stones or garden figures.

HOW TO COLLECT FROM A LOSS

❖ Be sure you have photographs and a description of your collection in case of a robbery. Keep them in a safe place away from your house.

❖ If you're photographing antiques for insurance records, use a Polaroid camera or camcorder. There will be no negative and no one else has to see your treasures.

❖ If your home has just been robbed, don't immediately give the police a "complete" list of the stolen items and damage. Sit down later and make a detailed list. This police copy is the one your insurance company will use to settle any claims. Take photographs of the damage as soon as possible.

❖ If you are the victim of a theft, be sure to give the police complete information about your antiques. You should have a good description, a photograph, and any known identifying marks. You might want to send information and pictures of the stolen antiques to the local antiques papers.

❖ In case of a major theft, keep careful records. You may be able to deduct part of the uninsured loss from your income tax.

FIRE

❖ Have your chimney cleaned if you move into an old house or if you burn wood regularly. A creosote buildup can cause an explosion. Nesting animals can cause fire or smoke.

❖ Follow all the safety rules for fires that you were taught in school. A smoke alarm is mandatory in many cities and should be in every home near the kitchen, at the top of the stairs, and near bedrooms. Keep a handheld fire extinguisher in your kitchen, near paper collectibles, and near your books.

SALES AND MOVING VAN RULES

❖ If you are moving, be sure to get special insurance coverage for damage to your antiques. You may want valuable pieces covered by your insurance, not by the mover's policy.

Silver

Look for that lining

Storing

❖ Felt gives off hydrogen sulfide, which tarnishes silver. Do not use felt liners in drawers or felt bags to store silver unless they are the specially treated tarnish-preventive cloths.

❖ Use tarnish-preventive strips or cloth to keep silver from tarnishing in a closed cupboard.

❖ To store silver, wrap it in acid-free paper, then put it in a tarnish-preventive bag.

❖ Don't store silver in old newspapers. The ink will react with the metal and will slowly remove silver plating.

❖ If you put camphor (mothballs) in with the silver to prevent tarnish, don't let it touch the silver. Put the camphor in a wax paper cup.

❖ Rubber bands will stain silver through several layers of paper wrapping.

❖ When storing silver in an attic, remember that 97 degrees or more will melt the filler in some candlesticks. Heat speeds corrosion.

DISPLAY

❖ Silver is displayed best against a red background.

❖ Don't display silver on latex paint. It will tarnish quickly.

❖ Don't keep alcoholic beverages or perfume in silver containers. It will cause damage.

❖ To remove wax from silver candlesticks, put the candlesticks in the freezer for a few hours. The wax will freeze and peel off.

Or,

❖ Put candlesticks in the sink under hot running water until all the wax melts off. Then wash with mild soap and water.

REPAIRING

❖ To loosen a silver saltshaker lid that is stuck to the glass shaker, immerse the top in white vinegar. Soak overnight.

❖ If the hinge that holds the lid on a stein or other metal object is balky, try lubricating it with WD-40 (found in most hardware stores).

❖ If you break the handle on an old silver coffeepot, have it resoldered. That repair detracts little from the resale value, but a new handle lowers the value by 50 percent.

❖ Always repair dented silver. Repeated cleaning of a piece with a dent can eventually lead to a hole.

❖ An engraved monogram can be buffed off an old piece of silver by a competent jeweler or silversmith. But it is easier to tell friends that the strange initials on the platter are those of a great-great aunt. Removing the initial will lower the value. Never remove a coat of arms.

❖ Don't have old Sheffield silver replated. You can replate wares that were originally electroplated, but 18th-century Sheffield was made by fusing sheets of silver to copper. "Bleeding" Sheffield is worth more than replated Sheffield.

❖ To remove old protective lacquer from a piece of silver, immerse the piece in very hot water for a few hours. This should loosen the lacquer. The process may have to be repeated to get all of the lacquer off. You may have to try one of several commercial lacquer removers that are available.

CLEANING

❖ Discovered some very dirty old silver? Wash it with a brush in warm soapy water before you polish it. Dirt can scratch the silver.

❖ Don't mechanically buff silver. It will permanently change the color and wear away bits of the silver.

☛ *VALUE HINT*

When buying silver with bright cut design, avoid worn pieces. Best prices are paid for silver with clear, crisp designs.

❖ Wash silverware immediately after dinner. If this isn't possible, a quick rinse will help to remove food residues and avoid tarnish.

❖ Wash silver every time it is used. Before you polish silver on display, be sure to wash it to remove all dust. Small gritty pieces of dust will scratch the silver.

❖ Use a soft toothbrush to clean hard-to-reach spots on silver or jewelry.

❖ Clean silver with any acceptable commercial polish. Don't use household scouring powder on silver, no matter how stubborn the spot may be. Use a tarnish-retarding silver polish to keep your silver clean. It will not harm old solid or plated wares. Do not use "instant" silver polishes.

❖ Don't immerse a wooden handle, like those on a teapot or salad server, in water.

❖ Always dry silver immediately after using it. The chemicals in the water may stain.

❖ Never put silverware and stainless-steel flatware in the dishwasher basket together. The stainless can damage the silver.

❖ When polishing silver, first remove all detachable parts like screw-on handles or finials. Rest the silver piece on a cloth in your lap, never on the table or other hard surface. Polish by rubbing in circles. If there are wooden handles or other parts, these should be waxed when the silver is cleaned.

❖ To clean crevices in old silver, use a cotton-tipped cuticle stick.

❖ Don't clean the impressed hallmarks or names on the bottom of a piece of silver. You may eventually rub them off. Some collectors cover the marks on the bottom with cellophane tape to protect them.

❖ Be careful how you handle clean silver. Fingerprints will show and eventually tarnish.

❖ Flatware that is used regularly should be polished just once or twice a year.

❖ Clean silver with gilt, like berry spoons or salt dishes, with soap, warm water, and a sponge. Do not use abrasive polish.

☞ VALUE HINT

If there is gold wash in the bright cut silver design, the wash is a later addition. Victorian pieces were made with bright cutting against the gold to show the design in two colors.

❖Never clean niello (silver with incised design inlaid with a special black metal) with silver dips. It will ruin the piece.

THERE ARE DOZENS OF HOMEMADE SILVER POLISH SUGGESTIONS. HERE ARE A FEW.

❖ Silver polish can be made at home from a cup of cigar ashes, 2 tablespoons bicarbonate of soda, and enough water to make a paste. The only problem is finding a cigar smoker!

❖ The English use this old system for cleaning silver: Put the silver in a bowl, cover it with sour milk, and let it stand overnight. Rinse it in cold water the next morning; dry with a soft cloth.

❖ Toothpaste is a good emergency silver polish. Some say tartar-control brands are the best.

❖ It is said you can clean silver with a banana peel mashed in a blender.

❖ You can clean your silver with a thick paste of baking soda and water. Rub it on, rinse, wipe.

❖ We prefer the modern tarnish-preventing polishes. There is more time between cleanings.

More help in Metal chapter.

Textiles, Including Clothes

GETTING THE DIRT

❖ Fresh air and limited sunlight are good for fabrics. Cotton and linen should be washed once a year, even if stored in a drawer, because dirt will cause damage. Dry-clean wool and silk if cleaning is needed. Protect fabrics from moths with the usual precautions. Paradichlorobenzene will do the job.

❖ Wash your hands before handling old textiles.

❖ Clean old textiles before storing. Use moth sprays or mothballs regularly.

❖ Air old, musty textiles outdoors. Put them in the shade, protected from bird droppings.

❖ Old bed linens and tablecloths that have been stored for a long time should be soaked in water for at least 12 hours. This rehydrates the fibers and loosens any dirt or leftover soap.

CLOTHING

❖ Never hang a knit garment, one cut on the bias, or ornately beaded clothing. Store flat in an acid-free cardboard box.

❖ Don't hang valuable old dresses or jackets on hangers. This puts a strain on the shoulders. Vintage dresses and jackets can be hung on well-padded hangers. Store clothing flat or folded on a shelf, but do not let the fabric touch bare or painted wood.

❖ Stuff hats with acid-free tissue for storage. Make the stuffing deep enough so the hat brim does not touch the shelf.

❖ Dust a feather boa with a hair dryer set on cool.

❖ Remember, the original color of old fabrics may be an off-white color or ivory, not the gleaming white we see in modern fabrics.

❖ Don't send out your antique white linen or cotton items to be dry-cleaned. The chemicals will yellow the fabric. If possible, remove any rusty metal snaps or hooks, then boil the item for about 15 minutes in a weak solution of water and dry bleach or hand-wash it in soap, nonchlorine bleach, and tepid water. Be sure to rinse until all soap is removed. Dry naturally, not in a dryer, then iron.

Or,

❖ Presoak old linens and cottons in a mixture of one part glycerin from the drugstore and four parts water. Stains and discolorations will wash out more easily.

Or,

❖ Clean old linens the old way. Boil the linens and detergent in a pot on the stove for about 20 minutes. This should whiten them. Hang them out in the sun to dry.

Or,

❖ There are many recipes for whitening old textiles. Try the old-fashioned cure: a vinegar rinse. Mix one part white vinegar with four parts warm water.

Or,

❖ To remove yellowing and stains from old textiles, soak them in false-teeth cleaner and water mixed according to the directions on the package. Rinse several times. (Test a small piece of the fabric before you try this.)

Or,

❖ Soiled white quilts or fabrics in good condition can be helped. Soak the textile in the washing machine in a solution of warm water and 1 cup or more of powdered dishwasher detergent for 1 hour. Then put on the gentle wash cycle for a few minutes. Rinse thoroughly.

Or,

❖ Age-yellowed linens can be whitened the modern way. Soak the material overnight in a solution of nonchlorine bleach ($\frac{1}{2}$ cup dry oxygen bleach mixed in 2 gallons water). Use a plastic, glass, or stainless-steel tub. Remove any obvious stains with a stain-removing laundry spray. Then wash in hot soapy water and rinse in warm water. If possible, lay the textile on the grass to dry.

❖ Be sure to rinse fabrics until all soap residue is gone. Soap in the textile will scorch when you iron. Use distilled water for the final rinse.

❖ Old linens can be bleached occasionally, but frequent bleaching will weaken the fabric. Never use chlorine bleach.

❖ To remove rust spots from washable textiles, try Grandma's remedy: Boil the fabric in a solution of 4 teaspoons cream of tartar in 1 pint water.

Or,

❖ Rub lemon juice and salt on rust spots on white textiles. Then put the cloth in the sun.

❖ Try Grandma's solution to yellowing fabrics. She used bluing in the next to last rinse to cover the slight yellowing of age. Bluing is still sold at the supermarket.

❖ If you want to remove a grease stain from silk, wool, or paper, cover it with grated chalk. Cover the chalk with a piece of a brown paper bag. Set a warm iron on the paper. Repeat if necessary. Be sure the iron is not hot enough to scorch the paper.

❖ Never wash a colored textile without talking to an expert. Most of the old colors run and the fabric will ruined.

❖ Wash small handkerchiefs in a salad spinner. Put in the handkerchief, soap, and water, spin, then rinse and spin again.

❖ Fabrics decorated with metal threads should not be washed. Wipe metallic designs with a cotton swab and ammonia.

❖ Gold or silver lace may tarnish. Sometimes it can be cleaned by rubbing it with a brush dipped in warm white wine.

❖ If your chairs have needlepoint seats, be careful when cleaning. Cover the seat with a piece of netting when you vacuum so the threads will not be pulled.

IRONING

❖ If you scorch a textile while ironing, try this old trick: Rub a cut onion over the scorch, then soak the cloth in cold water for 1 hour. Rewash and then iron.

❖ Use a clean plant mister to dampen old fabrics for ironing. Mist the cloth, then roll it and wrap it in a towel for a few hours so the moisture will be absorbed into the threads. Or you may be able to find an old-fashioned sprinkler bottle to hold the water to dampen the clothes.

❖ When ironing old fabrics, protect the delicate pieces by putting them between two pieces of an old sheet.

❖ The embroidery on linens and dresses should be raised. Iron properly or it will flatten. Put the embroidery face down on a soft towel, then press.

❖ Never hang antique clothing on wire coat hangers. Use padded hangers.

❖ Don't use a steam iron on old linens.

❖ Lace handkerchiefs can be pressed the old-fashioned way. After washing the handkerchief, push it flat on a mirror or tile wall surface. Straighten it, let the water run off and the handkerchief dry. It will need no further ironing. Avoid using an iron. It will flatten the lace.

❖ If you have old laces and ribbons, press them by pulling them over a warm electric light bulb. Limp lace can be washed, then sprayed with starch or sizing. Lace can be colored beige by a quick dip in tea.

STORAGE

❖ Never store textiles on or in paper, cardboard, or unsealed wood. Store in unbleached muslin. Wooden drawers and cardboard boxes contain acids and resins that can harm textiles.

❖ Old linens should be rolled, not folded. Creases weaken the fabric. If storing over a long period, do not starch. Starch attracts silverfish. Quilts can be folded.

❖ Moths can damage stored textiles. Use moth crystals

such as paradichlorobenzene. The vapors are heavier than air, so the crystals or mothballs must be placed above the textiles, preferably in small cloth bags suspended from the ceiling.

❖ Hanging textiles should be given a rest from time to time. The weight of the hanging causes strain on the threads. If the textile is taken down and stored for a few months, the threads will regain some strength.

❖ Never hang an antique fabric on a line to dry. The weight of the wet fabric could tear it. Lay it flat on towels.

Quilts

❖ "A stitch in time" is good advice. Always repair a torn quilt immediately to avoid further damage.

❖ Although coverlets and blankets should be rolled for storage, quilts should be folded.

❖ If you have stored a quilt, twice each year take it out and refold it—in half if you had it in thirds before. This will avoid crease lines.

☛ *VALUE HINT*

Hold quilts, coverlets, or bandannas to the light to find the holes and weak spots before you buy.

❖ A quilt that is not in use should be aired each year. Open up and put flat on the floor or a bed for a few days. A quilt that is used on a bed or hung should be taken down and rested every six months.

❖ Don't attach Velcro to a quilt to hang it. It will cause the fabric to discolor or rot. Use a muslin sleeve stitched to the quilt.

FURS

❖ Furs should never be stored in sealed plastic bags. They need to breathe.

❖ Brush fur in the direction it grows. If brushed the other way, the hairs will break off.

❖ Old furs oxidize and change color. Dark furs darken, light furs turn yellow, brown furs often turn reddish brown.

UMBRELLAS

❖ Store parasols and umbrellas closed.

You might find more in the Advertising and Rugs chapters.

Tools

❖ Some collectors want tools in restored condition. Others want a used look and think restoring lowers the value. If you want restored, cleaned tools, wash wood with Murphy's Oil Soap, dry, sand with steel wool, apply two coats of Minwax or other oil, then use paste wax and buff. Clean metal parts, then coat with clear lacquer.

❖ It's O.K. to repair obviously broken parts, tighten screws, and lightly wash wood and metal to remove built-up dirt if you don't want to do a major restoration. But don't coat the wood or metal with wax, varnish, oil, or other coatings that won't wash off.

The Wood and Metal chapters may have more information.

Tortoiseshell

THE SHELL GAME

❖ To polish tortoiseshell, rub it with a mixture of jeweler's rouge and olive oil, or rub it with a cloth dipped in lemon juice and salt. Rinse it with cold water; dry. Sometimes rubbing yogurt on the shell will help.

❖ Never store tortoiseshell combs or pins in plastic bags. The lack of air will cause the shell to crack or fade.

Toys and Banks

HAVE FUN WITH TOYS

❖ Don't repaint old metal toys. It lowers the value.

☛ *VALUE HINTS*

Rusted toys have very low value.

Reproduction cast-iron toys usually are heavier and thicker than the originals. The bottoms can be very different from those of old ones.

❖ To clean lithographed tin banks, try using Sani-wax (found at hardware stores) and 0000-grade steel wool, but use with extreme caution. Too much rubbing will remove all of the design.

❖ Remove the batteries from a stored toy.

☛ *VALUE HINT*

Take batteries with you to toy sales if you plan to buy a battery-operated toy. That way, you can check to see if the toy really works.

❖ Restoration of an old dollhouse should be restrained. Wash it, repair the structural problems, repaint as little as possible, and redecorate with appropriate old wallpaper fabrics and paint colors.

❖ If you have a battery-operated 1940s toy such as "Smoking Grandpa," you might want to replenish the smoke-maker when it wears out. Just put a few drops of sewing machine oil into the smoking tube. An electric spark in the toy causes the oil to smoke, and allows the toy to puff on a cigarette, pipe, or cigar.

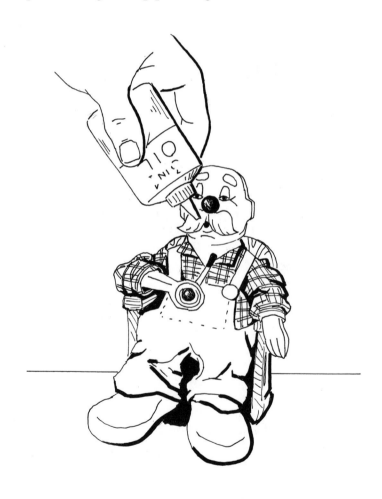

TEDDY BEARS

❖ If an old teddy bear needs washing, do it very carefully. First vacuum the fur, then mix water and liquid detergent and brush the detergent through the fur. Dry with a towel, then a hair dryer on low. Let dry completely; comb with a dog comb. Don't soak the bear if you don't have to. Some new bears are made to go through washing machine cycles.

❖ If you buy an old teddy bear that has been stored in a basement or garage, be sure to treat it for insect infestation. Put the bear in a box with a stick insecticide and seal the box for 60 hours.

There are more suggestions in the chapters about Advertising and Dolls.

Trunks

❖ Fill the trunk with fresh grass clippings. Close it. Stir each day for a week. The chlorophyll from the grass should absorb the smell, but watch the grass to be sure it doesn't rot.

❖ Another suggestion to remove the musty smell from an old trunk: Put a bowl of freshly ground coffee inside.

Or,

❖ Musty odors in trunks seem to be a constant problem. Try this system: Fill the trunk with wrinkled, crushed newspaper, close the lid for a week, remove and replace the papers. Repeat the process until the musty odor is gone. This system also helps with musty books if kept in a closed paper bag, and with suitcases.

Or,

❖ Open the trunk and let it air out in the sunlight.

Or,

❖ Try some of the commercial products found in hardware stores. Several new types claim to remove odors by filtering the air.

❖ If none of these work, try sealing the interior wood with a thin coat of varnish.

Furniture chapter suggestions will help you care for the outside of a trunk.

Wood

You would want to keep wood in good shape

❖ Wooden boxes, toys, or decoys should not be kept on the fireplace mantel or nearby floor area when the fire is burning. The heat dries the wood and the paint. Unprotected wooden items on warm TV sets and stereos may also be damaged.

❖ Wooden items should be kept off a sunny windowsill. Direct sunlight will harm wood finishes.

❖ When cleaning small wooden pieces, use the foam from a mixture of 1 tablespoon soap to 1 quart water. Whip the mixture with a beater and clean with the foam.

❖ If you use an old wooden bowl for salad, treat it with edible oil like walnut oil, not a furniture polish.

❖ Never use olive oil to treat a wooden bowl. It will turn rancid. If you used an olive oil–based salad dressing in the bowl at a meal, be sure to rinse the bowl.

❖ Don't store wooden bowls and other pieces on their sides. This can cause them to warp.

❖ To remove the odor from a wooden bowl, try airing it in sunlight after washing it with baking soda or vinegar. Soak the bowl for about 15 minutes, rinse with full-strength vinegar, then clear water. As a last resort, use diluted household bleach. If this does not remove the odor, repeat the process with a stronger solution of bleach.

The Furniture chapter has more help.

RELAX AND . . .

❖ Use and enjoy your antiques and collectibles. That's why you own them.

Product Sources

Check local hardware and art supply stores. Listed here are souces for a few items that might be hard to find.

Bestine solvent
available in art supply stores.
Union Rubber, Inc.
P.O. Box 1040
Trenton, NJ 08606
800-334-8219

Childproof locks
available in hardware stores.
"Tot-Lok" brand is manufactured by Rev-a-shelf
P.O. Box 99585
Louisville, KY 40269-0585
502-499-5835

Jeweler's rouge
ask retail jeweler for a local jewelry store supplier.
Colman-Borel
1812 Huron Road
Suite 600
Cleveland, OH 44115
216-861-2290
Rolite Chemical
596 Progress Drive
Hartland, WS 53029
414-367-2711

Liquid Wrench
available in hardware stores.
Radiator Specialty Co.
Charlotte, NC 28234-6080
704-377-6555

Minwax
available in hardware stores.
Minwax
50 Chestnut Ridge Road
Montville, NJ 07645
201-391-0253

Mylar bags and acid-free paper products
check in archival catalogs.
Exposures
41 S. Main Street
Norwalk, CT 06854
800-222-4947
Light Impressions
P.O. Box 940
Rochester, NY 14603-0940
800-828-6216
University Products, Inc.
517 Main Street
P.O. Box 101
Holyoke, MA 01041-0101
800-628-1912

Naval Jelly
available in hardware stores.
"Duro" brand is manufac-
tured by Loctite Corp.
4450 Cranwood Parkway
Cleveland, OH 44128
800-323-5106

Nevr-Dull
available in hardware stores.
George Basch Co.
P.O. Box 188
Freeport, NY 11520
516-378-8100

OxySolv rust remover
Solv-O Corp., Inc.
6995 Monroe Boulevard
Taylor, MI 48180
313-946-4440

Sani-wax
available in hardware stores.
Sani-wax Inc.
8340 Mission Road
Suite 118
Prairie Village, KS 66206
913-383-9703

Simichrome Metal Polish
available in hardware stores.
Competition Chemicals, Inc.
P.O. Box 820
Iowa Falls, IA 50126
515-648-5121

Softscrub
available in grocery stores.
Clorox Co.
P.O. Box 24305
Oakland, CA 94623
510-271-7000

Stick-em
Fox Run Craftman
1907 Stout Drive
Ivy Land, PA 18974
215-675-7700

**Tarnish-preventing silver
strips**
available in hardware stores.
Hagerty silver protection
strips made by W.J. Hagerty
& Sons Ltd., Inc.
P.O. Box 1496
South Bend, IN 46624
800-348-5162

Tri-Seal
Avalon Service and Supply
1624 Belmont Avenue
Chicago, IL 60657
312-525-2756

WD-40
available in hardware stores.
WD-40 Co.
1061 Cudahy
San Diego, CA 92110
619-275-1400

Index

Advertising , 1
Alabaster, 76–77
Albums, 1
Aluminum, 5, 69
Animal Trophies, 6

Bakelite, 64
Banks, 153
Barbie, 31–32
Basket, 10
Beads, 63, 66
Beer Can, 3
Billy Beer Cans, 2
Books, 11, 75
Bottles, 12, 54, 79
Brass, 15, 23
Bronze, 17, 88

Cabbage Patch Doll, 30
Candles, 18–19
Canning Jars, 13
Cans, 2, 4
Cards, 9
Carnival Glass, 55
Carousel Horses, 20
Celluloid, 114
Cels, 21
Chandelier, 73
Christmas, 57–58
Chrome, 22
Clock, 23–25
Clothes, 143–150
Coca-Cola, 2
Coffee Grinder, 68
Compacts, 88
Copper, 27
Cruets, 52, 55

Daguerreotype, 112–113
Dolls, 28–31
Drugs, 79
Dust, 6

Fans, 88
Fiesta Ware, 117
Fire, 136
Frame, 45
Furniture, 33–34, 36–37,
    39–42, 46–48
Furs, 150

Games, 49
Glass, 50–54
Golf Clubs, 84
Gorham, 27
Graniteware, 56
Grueby, 120
Guns, 91

Halloween, 57
Hardware, 15, 46
Heintz Art, 27
Holiday, 57
House Numbers, 130
Hummel, 26

Insects, 6, 30, 85
Insurance, 14, 26, 93–94,
    135, 136
Iron, 59, 68–69
Ivory, 17, 60, 65, 84, 88

Jade, 63–64
Jewelry, 62, 66–67
John Rogers Groups, 83

Key, 134
Kitchen, 68

Labels, 13, 82, 106
Lacquer, 71
Lamps, 72
Lead, 14
Leather, 74–75, 122
Light, 129
Lock, 131
Lusterware, 120

Marble, 76–77
Match Covers, 104
Medical, 79
Metal, 80
Mirrors, 44
Miscellaneous, 82
Molds, 27
Moths, 148
Moving , 93
Music, 95–96

Opals, 65

Paintings, 97–99
Paper, 87, 102–106
Paperweights, 107
Papier-mâche, 87
Pearl, 64–65
Pens, 110
Perfume Bottle, 51
Pewter, 110
Photographs, 88, 96, 113
Photography, 112
Pictures, 97, 100
Plastic, 114
Plate, 26
Poison, 27, 79
Political Button, 87
Porcelain, 116–121
Postcards, 103
Pottery, 116–121
Prints, 104

Product Sources, 161
Purses, 122

Quilts, 149

Radioactive, 79
Rhinestones, 62, 65
Rugs, 123–127
Rust, 3

Saddles, 75
Saltshaker, 80
Security, 128–136
Sicardo, 120
Signs, 2, 4
Silver, 81, 83, 120, 137–142
Snow Dome, 107–108
Soapstone, 84
Stove, 89
Sumida Ware, 120
Sundial, 8

Teddy Bear, 154–155
Textiles, 143–150
Thanksgiving, 57
Theft, 128, 136
Tiffany, 27, 73
Tintype, 112–113
Tools, 151
Tortoiseshell, 152
Toys, 153–155
Trade Cards, 1
Trench Art, 16
Trunks, 156–157

Umbrellas, 150

Water Spots, 39
White Rings, 38
Wicker, 43
Window, 8
Wood, 158–159
Wooden, 69